OZONE

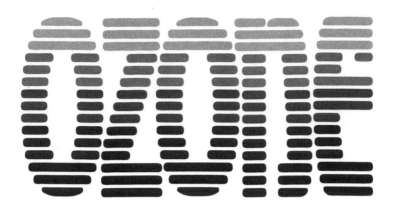

OZONE

BY
KATHLYN
GAY

Franklin Watts
New York / London / Toronto
Sydney / 1989
An Impact Book

Illustrations by: Vantage Art

All photographs courtesy of
Kathlyn Gay, except the following:
California Energy Commission:
p. 41; NASA: pp. 54, 67; RMI,
Robert Long, U.S. Navy: p. 65.

Library of Congress Cataloging-in-Publication Date

Gay, Kathlyn.
Ozone / by Kathlyn Gay.
p.   cm.—(An Impact book)
Bibliography: p.
Includes index.
Summary: Discusses the dual problem of too much ozone in the
troposphere creating smog and the depletion of the ozone layer in
the stratosphere which shields harmful ultraviolet rays.
ISBN 0-531-10777-9
1. Atmospheric ozone—Environmental aspects—Juvenile literature.
2. Ozone layer—Juvenile literature. 3. Chlorofluorocarbons—
Environmental aspects—Juvenile literature. [1. Ozone layer.
2. Ozone. 3. Air—Pollution.]   I. Title.
TD885.5.085G38   1989
363.73'92—dc20   89-9031   CIP   AC

CONTENTS

OZONE

OZONE— A HAZARD AND A BENEFIT

It is early morning in late August. The brownish haze hovering over a major urban center in the United States blocks some of the hot sunshine, but the temperature steadily climbs. The air feels so thick that, as some would say, "You could cut it with a knife." A radio broadcaster announces that "the air quality index for ozone is 193—in a range that could cause health problems." People with heart or respiratory ailments, such as asthma and hay fever, are advised to avoid physical activity outdoors—even walking can be harmful. "If the air quality index climbs to over 200, healthy people also should reduce their outdoor activity as much as possible," the reporter warns.

Later that same day, a news broadcaster makes another announcement about ozone. This time the story focuses on ozone in the stratosphere, a layer of air about 6 miles (10 km) to 30 miles (50 km) above the earth. Within the stratosphere, ozone creates a gaseous shield that protects the earth from the sun's ultraviolet (UV) radiation. The big news is that a recent experiment, one of many by atmospheric scientists, supports the theory that the protective ozone layer is thinning.

The dangers of losing some of the ozone shield and the hazards of ozone as an air pollutant have been of increasing concern. But just what is ozone?

A REACTIVE GAS

Wherever it occurs, ozone (O_3) is a colorless gas, a form of oxygen. However, an ordinary molecule of oxygen contains two atoms while a molecule of ozone contains three atoms ($O + O_2 \rightarrow O_3$). Because of ozone's composition, it is reactive. That is, it readily combines with and oxidizes (breaks down) whatever materials it comes in contact with, including such biological substances as cells and tissues.

Far above the earth, ozone forms naturally as oxygen produced from living things moves from the troposphere, the layer of air nearest the earth's surface, to the stratosphere. (Scientists label the layers of the atmosphere according to the way temperature changes with altitude.) Air in the stratosphere absorbs solar energy, or heat from the sun, which in turn creates a photochemical reaction that produces ozone—a benefit to the environment since ozone protects people, plants, and animals from harmful radiation.

The gas also forms in the troposphere when sunlight strikes nitrogen oxides (NO_x) and hydrocarbons (HCs)—compounds of hydrogen and carbon—and other volatile organic compounds (VOCs) that come from a variety of industries, vehicle exhausts, and consumer products. As the nitrogen oxides and hydrocarbons "stew" in the sun, the reaction that takes place produces ozone, the main ingredient in the pollutant commonly known as "smog."

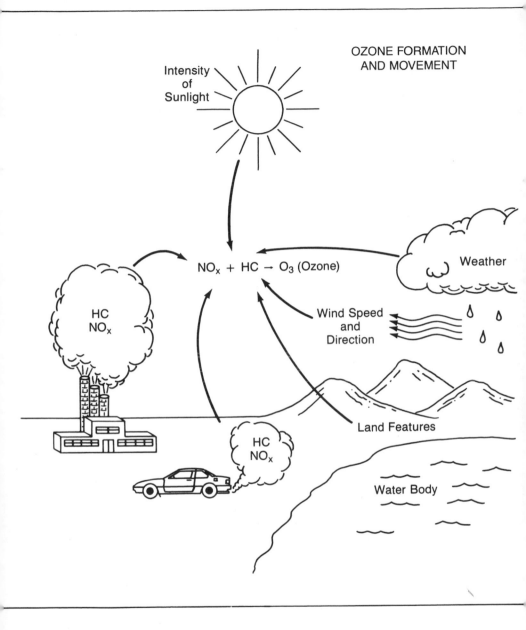

OZONE FORMATION
AND MOVEMENT

Intensity
of
Sunlight

NO_x + HC → O_3 (Ozone)

HC
NO_x

Weather

Wind Speed
and
Direction

Land Features

HC
NO_x

Water Body

*Ozone is formed when hydrocarbons
(HC) and nitrogen oxide (NOx) react
to heat and sunlight. Its movement is
affected by weather and geography.*

Biogenic or naturally produced hydrocarbons (NHCs) formed by trees and other vegetation in the presence of nitrogen oxides and sunlight also can produce ozone, but until recently it was generally believed that NHCs played only a small part in urban smog episodes. However, in a recent study of Atlanta's air, a group of researchers from the School of Geophysical Sciences at the Georgia Institute of Technology found that "NHC emissions appear to be as large as, if not larger than" anthropogenic or human-produced hydrocarbons (AHCs). The scientific team also pointed out that NHCs react faster than AHCs, so they "can have a significant effect" even in low concentrations, and concluded that NHCs must be considered when developing strategies to control smog.[1]

Although NHCs could contribute to ozone pollution in some urban areas, most programs to deal with smog have concentrated on reducing human-produced nitrogen oxides and carbon monoxide (CO), another ingredient in smog, from motor vehicles as well as VOCs from manufacturing plants. These air pollutants have increased rapidly over the past few decades with the growth in industry and transportation, creating health hazards for people in many urban areas of the United States and other industrialized nations.

DIFFERENT PROBLEMS; COMMON TIES

The dual ozone problems—pollution or smog in the troposphere and depletion of the ozone layer in the stratosphere—are very different. But the problems have common ties in that they both are related to air pollutants that come from industry, transportation, and other human activities.

Although ozone depletion in the stratosphere is a relatively recent problem, air pollution that contributes to a variety of environmental hazards is not a new concern. Since the time of the industrial revolution in the 1800s, people in many urban areas of the world have suffered from "dirty air." As the number of coal- and oil-burning power plants, factories, steel mills, foundries, and other manufacturing and processing plants increased, smoke, soot, and other particulates spewed into the air. Exhaust fumes from more and more cars and trucks added to the pollution problem. Chemical processing plants, waste disposal facilities, pesticides, and herbicides have been responsible for adding more pollutants—some of them highly toxic—to the atmosphere.

By the mid-1900s, air pollution was considered a major threat to the environment and human health. Instances of "smoggy air" occurred more and more frequently over major urban centers from London to New York to Los Angeles to Tokyo. Many of these smog covers were (and still are) brought on by thermal inversion. That is, cold air, which is more dense than warm air, settles near the ground, frequently at night. If there is no wind or rain, warm air forms a stationary "lid" above the cold air and pollutants near the ground cannot disperse. Instead, they "cook" in the sunlight until winds or rains break up the layers of air. Los Angeles, built in a basinlike valley, often suffers from an inversion, and the surrounding mountains help trap smog over the city for days at a time.

London, England also is frequently plagued with smog. However, the development of smog in London does not necessarily come about because of photochemical reactions—hydrocarbons and nitrogen oxides stewing in the sun. Rather, London-type smog usually occurs when moisture from fog and heavy dew condenses on smoke particles that contain sulfur dioxide (SO_2), a colorless and toxic gas and also a component in acid rain. London experienced one of the world's worst smog events during a week in December 1952 when at least 4,000 people died from smog-related respiratory diseases.

EFFORTS TO CLEAN UP
AIR POLLUTION

A number of major cities around the world have passed laws requiring controls on sources of air pollutants. In the United States, cities like Los Angeles and Pittsburgh began air cleanup efforts during the 1960s. The federal government also passed a Clean Air Act and amended it in 1970 to set standards for safe amounts of carbon monoxide, carbon dioxide, nitrogen oxides, ozone, lead, and particulates such as soot and dust allowed in ambient air (concentrations of air over a particular community). In 1970, Congress also set up the Environmental Protection Agency (EPA), which is responsible for enforcing regulations that protect the environment.

An important part of the 1970 Clean Air Act was an order for states to develop programs for reducing ozone levels to no more than 0.08 parts of ozone per million parts of ambient air (ppm). The law stated that the ozone level should not be exceeded more than one day a year. However, states were unable to meet the standards and in 1979 the EPA raised the level to 0.12 ppm. Health standards set by the Clean Air Act and its amendments, along with measures enacted by states and cities, went a long way to help improve air quality. As an example, Pittsburgh was once blanketed with smoke and smog that cut off daylight. But emissions from steel mills, foundries, rail yards, and other sources were brought under control so that Pittsburgh has become a more livable city.

Overall, the nation's air has been getting much cleaner over the past few decades. According to EPA data for the period 1976–1985, emissions and concentration levels of such air pollutants as lead, nitrogen dioxide (NO_2), sulfur dioxide, and carbon monoxide dropped considerably. Even the number of peak ozone periods per year have decreased, and most areas of the country have made solid gains in controlling ozone pollution. But there also has been economic expansion, which is accompanied by emissions from industry and additional cars and trucks on the roads. This offsets the gains and in some areas has contributed to a slow rise in air pollutants. In fact, many urban centers across the country are now violating clean air standards.

Controversy over the need for increased environmental protection has erupted time and again during the 1980s. Some politicians, manufacturers, business leaders, and others want to slow down efforts to clean up the environment. Critics of government regulations argue that pollution-abatement measures are so expensive to apply that industries must close or cut back production, thus forcing workers from their jobs.

Environmentalists, on the other hand, insist that the general public is deeply concerned about pollution, whether it produces smog, causes loss of the ozone shield, acid rain, or the "greenhouse effect" (a forced warming of the earth), or contaminates soils or waterways. According to public opinion expert Louis Harris, poll after poll during the 1980s showed that "when it comes down to choosing between health and jobs . . . the American people will opt by a wide margin for health."[2] Harris polls also showed that Americans are willing to pay increased taxes to control pollution. However, no one can be sure how the opinions will translate

into action if people lose income or actually must pay higher taxes.

Realistically, what are some trade-offs that Americans and people in other industrialized nations have to make in order to protect themselves and their environment? What are the possible consequences of not reducing levels of ozone and other air pollutants? What is being done to stop the loss of beneficial ozone in the stratosphere?

These are just a few of the questions raised and discussed in the next chapters. The effects of smog and efforts to reduce ozone pollution are covered first because the problems have a longer history and attempted solutions have been underway for more than two decades. In addition, ozone pollution, which is usually local in nature, leads to the broader issue of air pollution worldwide that may be creating climate changes as well as depleting the ozone shield. Protecting life on the planet could begin with cleaning up the air over major urban centers, at home and abroad.

Heavy hangs the haze over Indianapolis, Indiana. Like many urban centers in the United States and other parts of the world, the city suffers episodes of smog. Because of emissions from industries and motor vehicles, many cities do not meet clean air standards set by the U.S. Environmental Protection Agency (EPA).

EFFECTS
OF OZONE
POLLUTION

Not all areas of the United States or other industrialized nations suffer from intense episodes of smog, so why has ozone pollution become a major environmental issue? In the first place, ozone pollution adversely affects the health of far more people—between 75 and 100 million Americans—than does other types of air pollution. Most smog problems occur in areas with large populations, such as the urban area called the Eastern Corridor along the Atlantic coast of the United States. Extending from Maine to Virginia, the corridor includes Boston, New York City, Philadelphia, and Washington, D.C.

Second, smog can spread from a large urban center to the surrounding countryside. The coastal city of Ventura, California, and its surrounding county, for example, are northwest of Los Angeles, well beyond the mountains that rim the Los Angeles basin and hold in its smog. But when the winds carry ozone pollution out of the basin, some of the smog moves into Ventura

County. With ozone levels measuring 0.18 ppm on some days, Ventura County is ranked by the EPA as among the worst in the nation for dirty air, following the New York–New Jersey area (0.19 ppm), Houston (0.20 ppm), and Los Angeles (0.35 ppm).

NATURE OF THE PROBLEM

Not all of the smog in Ventura County slips in from Los Angeles, however, and this points up some of the varied elements that contribute to ozone-polluted air. Widespread population growth accompanied by a large increase in motor vehicles has added to the smog problem. In addition, one area of the county has a mini-valley similar to the Los Angeles basin where ozone pollution is trapped.

Geography is a major factor in ozone pollution, with mountain ranges trapping ozone in valley regions. But wind and climate patterns also affect the production of ozone. Since sunshine is needed to produce smog, sunny areas like the southeast and southwest United States may suffer from smog episodes at any time of the year if air circulation is poor and other conditions favor the production of ozone. But in most parts of the nation, ozone pollution is a summer problem because of the increase in sunshine and the warm, stagnant air that hovers over metropolitan areas.

Yet the primary causes of ozone pollution are the large industrial complexes and transportation systems that have developed since the mid-1900s. The highest concentration of industry and motor vehicles is in major cities where there are many thousands of sources for "precursor emissions"—hydrocarbons and nitrogen oxides that will create the by-product ozone.

In the United States, motor vehicles produce

Traffic congestion adds to air pollution problems in many cities across the U.S. VOCs from motor vehicle emissions help create smog, acid rain, and depletion of ozone in the stratosphere.

nearly seven million metric tons of VOCs each year, one-third of the total VOC emissions annually. Motor vehicles are also a major source of nitrogen oxides.

A major portion of the annual VOC emissions comes from many thousands of stationary sources, such as power plants, spray-painting companies, chemical and petroleum refineries, gasoline-storage terminals, dry-cleaning plants, breweries, bakeries, chemical manufacturers, and waste disposal facilities. In addition, precursors come from countless consumer products such as household cleaners and deodorants.

The nature of the ozone pollution problem is complicated even further by the recent findings that biogenic hydrocarbons in rural areas may play an important role in ozone production if nitrogen oxide is present. Since it is impossible to control hydrocarbon emissions from natural sources, it will be necessary to more strictly control human-produced hydrocarbons as well as nitrogen oxide emissions. Another complicating factor is the varied rates at which precursors move and react in the atmosphere. In order to find ways to significantly reduce ozone pollution, the experts will need to know how the transport and mixing of precursors affect ozone levels.

HEALTH HAZARDS

The air-monitoring equipment installed in the Glendora schools of Los Angeles County began to emit shrill signals. Children on the playgrounds quickly lined up to go inside the buildings. Most of the youngsters were well aware that the heavy smog, which had blanketed the area, would be dangerous to their health. In fact, some children were already complaining of burning eyes, and others were coughing and wheezing.

High levels of ozone pollution can trigger a number of respiratory problems. But long-term exposure to ozone pollution may pose an even greater health risk, according to one study conducted for a three-month period during 1984. A research team from the University of Southern California's School of Medicine measured lung function of more than a thousand second- and fifth-grade students in Los Angeles and compared the results with tests of children in a less-polluted area of the country. Researchers found that "long-term exposure to relatively low levels of air pollution may be far more dangerous to growing children than occasional exposure to peak pollution levels."

For the testing, children blew into an instrument called a spirometer. Measurements from the instrument indicate a person's lung size and the airflow in the large and small passageways of the lungs. Oxygen from inhaled air is transported in the lungs via a complex system of airways that divide and narrow, and then is sent to the bloodstream via tiny air sacs. Cells in both the airways and air sacs are sensitive to and can be damaged by ozone.

The Los Angeles children suffered some damage in the lung airways, which were thickened by air pollutants and increased secretions. Essentially, this reduces lung function so that "it takes more energy to breathe," the director of the study group reported. The study suggested that the growth of the lungs could be inhibited. Lung function, which deteriorates as people stop growing, also could deteriorate at an earlier age for Los Angeles children than for those who are not exposed to long-term pollution during their growing years.

Other studies also have shown that exposure to ozone as low as the legally allowed standard of 0.12 ppm interferes with the normal functioning of the lung. According to an EPA report, a series of experiments was conducted using a controlled environmental chamber where people with healthy lungs were exposed to ozone for one to three hours. Heavy exercise during this ozone exposure reduced "normal functioning of the lung by 10 percent or more in about 5 to 20 percent of subjects, including both adults and children."[3]

In the same series of studies, healthy people exposed to ozone concentration levels from 0.12 ppm to greater than 0.20 ppm experienced "chest pain, coughing, wheezing, pulmonary and nasal congestion, labored breathing, sore throat, nausea, and faster respiratory rate. The severity of these effects appears to be dose related. . . ." In other words, as ozone levels increased, more people were affected and more pain and discomfort were reported.

A study conducted at a YMCA summer camp in Fairview Lake, New Jersey also showed changes in lung function of children exposed to levels of ozone even lower than the standard set by the EPA. Although the children at the summer camp and those involved in other studies experienced only short-term effects from ozone pollution, repeated exposure could lead to chronic respiratory problems, researchers believe.[4]

Studies with animals have confirmed that ozone not only initiates damage to sensitive lung tissue, but also that the damage continues for some time after ozone exposure has ended. As the National Wildlife Federation (NWF) noted: "If the exposure is not repeated, the damaged tissue repairs itself, leaving a small amount of scar tissue. If the exposure is repeated or continued for long periods of time, scar tissue can become extensive enough to cause permanent lung damage."

The animal studies also showed that the immune system is affected by ozone. Some animals exposed to ozone levels as low as 0.08 ppm for short or long periods became susceptible to respiratory diseases—the animals had less resistance to infection.

WHO'S AT RISK?

"The evidence is overwhelming that ozone levels currently monitored in major metropolitan areas are unhealthy for the general population," the EPA has noted. The agency estimates that 20 million to 30 million people "potentially sensitive to ozone live in major urban areas where ozone levels are at least 25 percent above the current health standard."[5]

For most people, the effects of short-term exposure (one to two hours) to ozone may subside once they are out of the polluted environment—perhaps in an air-conditioned vehicle or building. But medical experts say there is some possibility that ozone pollution could create other health problems in the long-term, as the study with Los Angeles schoolchildren seemed to indicate. In addition, some groups of people face more ozone-related health risks than others. Those most in danger from air pollutants, according to the American Lung Association, are the elderly, infants, pregnant women, and victims of chronic lung and heart disease.

Exercisers make up another at-risk group, particularly those who exercise vigorously outdoors, such as joggers and bicyclists. When exercising, a person's breathing rate increases, which in turn allows more ozone to be carried to the sensitive parts of the lung. Health officials say that people should curtail vigorous exercise on days when air quality is poor, and sports events should be postponed. Not only do athletes risk lung damage, but research shows that their performance usually deteriorates with a rise in ozone levels. In fact, during the 1984 Los Angeles Olympics, city officials were so convinced that high ozone levels adversely affected athletic performance that they limited motor vehicle use and took other special measures to make sure that athletes would not be hampered by smog.

Construction workers and others in urban areas who have no choice but to work outdoors also may face more health risks from ozone-polluted air than those who have indoor jobs. However, in some workplaces and homes, indoor air can be polluted with many other hazardous substances.[6]

Limiting the time outdoors when ozone levels are high may be one of the only ways outdoor workers can provide some protection for themselves. Many people, whatever their occupations or leisure activities, try to find ways to restrict physical exertion outdoors during days when the air quality index shows a dangerous level of pollutants. Some runners, for example, have found that they develop breathing problems when ozone levels are high and may find a substitute activity such as a swim indoors or exercise in a gym.

EFFECTS OF OZONE
ON TREES AND PLANTS

Since the 1970s, the EPA, the U.S. Forest Service, the U.S. Department of Agriculture, and a number of other government agencies and environmental organizations have studied the effects of air pollution on various crops, trees, and other vegetation. Greenhouse experiments and field studies show that ozone is toxic to plants and destroys a variety of crops. In California alone, more than $300,000 in crops are lost each year due to smog damage.

One EPA study, the National Crop Loss Assessment Network (NCLAN), indicated that when ozone concentration during the growing season exceeds 0.04 ppm to 0.05 ppm, there is a 10 percent or more loss in the yield of such major cash crops as soybeans, peanuts, corn, and wheat. The NCLAN study also showed that ozone exposure

> can reduce plant yield in tomatoes 33 percent, beans 26 percent, soybeans 20 per-

cent, and snapbeans up to 22 percent. The potential crop losses alone are estimated at two billion to three billion dollars per year.[7]

Along with poor crop yields, forest damage can be traced to air pollutants, particularly ozone and acid deposition. Popularly known as acid rain, acidic deposits include dry and wet substances formed from gaseous sulfur and nitrogen oxides. Acid rain has been blamed for much tree and plant damage as well as the death of fish and plant life in lakes in northeastern United States, Canada, and some European countries.

To test the effects of ozone pollution, acidic deposits, and other air pollutants, plants inside laboratory chambers are sprayed with chemicals that produce smog or acid rain. The results are then recorded and analyzed.

However, some reviewers of scientific data insist that the evidence does not support the theory that acid rain causes damage to U.S. forests. For example, Richard L. Kerch, director of Air Quality Activities for Consolidation Coal Company in Pittsburgh, Pennsylvania, acknowledged that there is documented evidence of dying trees, particularly in northeastern U.S. forests, but he attributed this to primarily "climatic stress and forest pests."[8] This is usually the view stated by representatives of other coal companies and coal-burning power plants and industries whose smokestack emissions often contain sulfur dioxide, a precursor of acid rain.

Certainly, no one factor can be blamed for forest decline. Trees and plants can be damaged by a number of natural stresses such as viruses and insects and the amounts of moisture, extremes in temperatures (very hot and very cold), geographical locations, and injuries from storms and wildfires. But atmospheric scientist Volker A. Mohnen, who has been studying atmospheric processes that affect forests, has noted that "since 1980 many forests in the eastern U.S. and parts of Europe have suffered a drastic loss of vitality—a loss that could not be linked to any of the familiar causes, such as insects, disease or direct poisoning by a specific air or water pollutant. . . ." Finding a direct cause for forest damage can be elusive, however. Mohnen pointed out in a *Scientific American* article that although trees can suffer from a number of natural stresses and injuries, acid precipitation, ozone, and other air pollutants could add to the stresses and "handicap the trees," leading to forest decline.[9]

The Health Task Force of the American Forestry Association reviewed scientific studies of forest-health threats and concluded that anthropogenic substances such as air pollutants are just as hazardous as—or perhaps more threatening than—natural stresses to various species of trees, especially conifers (evergreens). "Ozone, for example, has been proven to cause injury and mortality of eastern white pine and injury to white fir, ponderosa pine, and other trees in the mountains of Southern California," the Task Force noted.[10]

An earlier laboratory study report, published in *Science* magazine, pointed out that ozone may "cause the greatest amount of damage to vegetation of any gaseous pollutant." According to findings from the laboratory study, ozone reduced the rates of photosynthesis, the process by which plants capture and use solar energy, in several species of trees and crops. The researchers were unable to determine the process by which ozone reduces photosynthesis. But evidence clearly showed that reduced photosynthesis brought on by ozone exposure diminished tree growth and crop yields.[11]

More recent studies of air pollution effects on vegetation show that ozone and acid deposition *together* pose considerable threat to trees such as conifers. As a West German scientist, Bernhard Prinz, explained in an article on possible causes of forest damage in Europe: "Ozone affects the trees' energetic metabolism in a direct way and also weakens the cell membrane system so that, in combination with acid rain and fog, the leaching of essential nutrients is enhanced. As a further result, the root system is affected and the uptake of

Dead or dying trees are often the result of stress brought on by ozone in combination with acid rain.

nutrients from the soil is reduced. . . ." Prinz concluded that short-term damage to conifers in Europe is probably due to climatic conditions, but the most probable causes of long-term damage involve "the upward trend of ozone concentration during the last few decades and the continuous loss of nutrients in soil by acid deposition."[12]

OTHER EFFECTS

Because of its reactive nature, ozone also can damage manufactured goods and natural building materials. For example, it causes rubber to crack, dyes to fade, and paint to erode. In combination with acidic deposits, it is responsible for corrosion of metal, concrete, and stone, particularly limestone, in various structures such as bridges, monuments, and statues.

Most of the research on how ozone affects non-biological materials was conducted several decades ago, so continued study is necessary to determine the costs of ozone-induced damage to metals and other manufactured materials. But research on materials damage as well as continued study of the health effects of ozone pollution are not the only actions needed to solve the problem of dirty air across the nation. Solutions to the ozone pollution problem in the United States depend on cooperation between business and government, enforcement of federal and state laws, and individual efforts to control pollutants.

CONTROLLING OZONE PRECURSORS

The deadline was August 31, 1988. At that time, more than seventy U.S. cities and counties, which had not yet met standards for legal levels of ozone and other air pollutants, were to be in compliance with the 1979 amendments to the federal Clean Air Act. The 1979 legislation required cities to attain the National Ambient Air Quality Standards (NAAQS) for ozone and carbon monoxide by 1982. But when urban areas could not meet the 1982 deadline, the EPA granted extensions until the end of 1987.

Once more, however, the harmful air pollutants were not brought under control. Again the EPA extended the deadline. But there were still dozens of "nonattainment" areas, as the EPA calls them, by the end of August 1988. That summer's heat wave, which broke high-temperature records across the nation, added to air pollution problems, creating "yellow alerts"—smog episodes that threatened the health of New Yorkers, Chicagoans, and people in many other major cities.

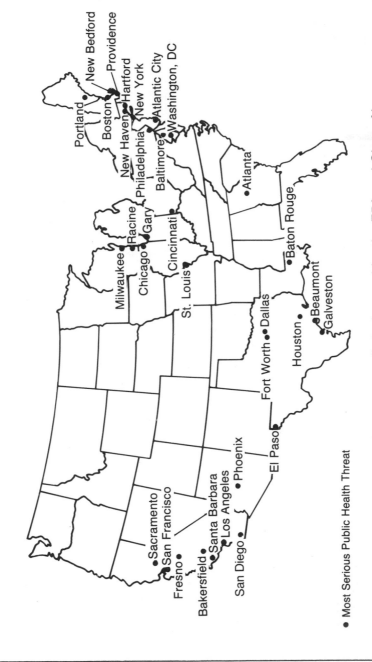

Portland
New Bedford
Providence
Boston
Hartford
New Haven
New York
Philadelphia
Baltimore
Atlantic City
Washington, DC

Atlanta

Baton Rouge

Racine
Gary
Milwaukee
Chicago
Cincinnati

St. Louis

Dallas
Fort Worth
Houston
Beaumont
Galveston

El Paso

Sacramento
San Francisco
Fresno
Bakersfield
Santa Barbara
Los Angeles
Phoenix
San Diego

● Most Serious Public Health Threat

"Ozone nonattainment areas" designated by the EPA and Clean Air
Coalition groups, shown here in a map that indicates the cities
whose air pollution problems pose a serious threat to public health.

Why have urban areas been unable to comply with federal regulations for air quality? What penalties, if any, do cities and counties face for noncompliance with the Clean Air Act? Who is responsible for setting up programs to control ozone and other pollutants?

PROVISIONS OF THE CLEAN AIR ACT

According to the Clean Air Act, the EPA is charged with enforcing NAAQS. In the case of the ozone standard, an area exceeds the limit if the ozone reading is over 0.12 ppm for more than one hour per day. For tail pipe emissions from passenger cars, the limits are expressed in grams per mile (gpm). For example, the standard for carbon monoxide is 3.4 gpm. In 1988, the standard for nitrogen oxide was 1.0 gpm and 0.4 gpm for hydrocarbons, but some federal lawmakers would like to cut those limits by more than one-half.

The law requires that each state submit a plan to control air pollutants and identify the geographic areas that exceed the health standards for ozone and carbon monoxide. The EPA must approve each state's plan or help a state set up a plan that would meet its approval. Each state must then apply the rules and regulations to attain the standards and also prevent its industries from polluting the air of other states.

If a state does not make "reasonable efforts" to implement its plan to control air pollutants, the Clean Air Act requires that the EPA impose severe economic sanctions (penalties) on the nonattainment cities or areas within that state. Those penalties include bans on construction of new industry and withholding federal funds for highway, sewer, and water projects.

Over the years, the EPA has imposed penalties on only a dozen or so urban areas, including Chicago and

Los Angeles. The agency believes that sanctions should be used only when an area has shown reluctance to carry out a plan for reducing ozone and carbon monoxide levels. Thus penalties do not automatically apply to some nonattainment areas, especially if they have put into effect some control programs.

APPLYING PENALTIES

Uncertainties about the long-range transport of ozone-producing pollutants also adds to the difficulty of applying penalties for not meeting federal ozone standards. As one U.S. government study put it:

> Wind can transport ozone and its associated chemical compounds for miles both during and after transformation, causing high concentrations in other areas. How far winds can move ozone, however, is uncertain. Therefore, it is very difficult to predict where and to what extent ozone and ozone-forming chemicals will raise ozone levels in specific areas.[13]

In late 1986, U.S. senators and representatives from the state of Wisconsin requested that the U.S. General Accounting Office (GAO) investigate the question of ozone transport across state lines. The GAO is an independent agency within the federal government that assists Congress in overseeing and auditing various government programs and makes recommendations for more efficient government services. Because ozone levels were high in several Wisconsin counties, Wisconsin officials charged that ozone pollution from the northwestern Indiana and Chicago areas prevented Wisconsin from attaining the health standard for ozone.

The Wisconsin delegation claimed that Illinois and Indiana had not developed the required regulations for controlling ozone-producing emissions in some counties bordering Lake Michigan.

The GAO conducted an investigation from January through November 1987. In the process, the GAO reviewed pollution control laws in the states, interviewed officials of pollution control agencies and directors of EPA regional offices, and discussed with experts the various computer models for measuring ozone levels and ozone transport.

What were the findings? EPA officials had not been able to determine the exact extent to which Illinois and Indiana contribute to Wisconsin's ozone problem. But federal and state environmental agencies were convinced that winds generally move ozone and its precursors in a northward direction along Lake Michigan. In addition, officials found that two Wisconsin counties did not have the emission sources that would result in high ozone levels. Thus industries in Chicago and northwestern Indiana, officials declared, contributed to ozone problems in two southern Wisconsin counties. However, the officials did not agree on whether Illinois and Indiana emissions affected a more northern county where the industrial city of Milwaukee is located. Apparently, emissions from industries in Milwaukee County could be responsible for high levels of ozone pollution over that area.

How, then, was the EPA to go about applying penalties for polluting the air with ozone precursors? In the case of the Illinois and Indiana counties that had violated ozone standards, the EPA imposed construction bans. That is, no factories could be modified and no new industries could be built if they would be major sources of ozone-forming pollutants. However, as in other in-

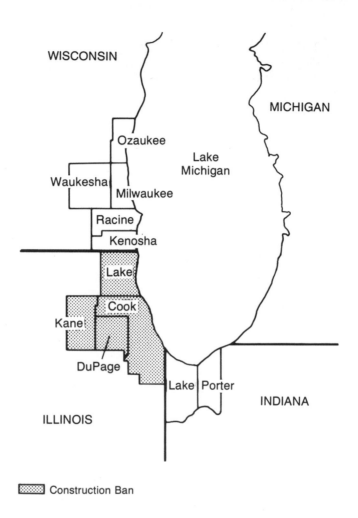

WISCONSIN

MICHIGAN

Ozaukee

Lake
Michigan

Waukesha

Milwaukee

Racine

Kenosha

Lake

Cook

Kane

DuPage

Lake Porter

INDIANA

ILLINOIS

▒▒▒ Construction Ban

*A 1987 audit conducted by the U.S. General Accounting
Office (GAO) revealed that industries in Chicago and
northwestern Indiana contributed to high levels of ozone
in southeastern Wisconsin. As a result, the EPA
imposed construction penalties on the Illinois and
Indiana counties that had violated ozone standards.*

stances in which the EPA has imposed a construction penalty, the ban would be lifted once the states adopted the regulations needed for air pollution control. In fact, EPA and state officials work together to develop pollution control plans that will meet the Clean Air Act requirements. As an EPA official explained, the agency "views the ban as a prod to get the states to produce good plans, not as a punishment for failing to meet air-quality standards."[14]

REDUCING EMISSIONS FROM MOBILE SOURCES

Many government officials and members of environmental groups have emphasized that one of the most important strategies for reducing ozone pollution is controlling emissions from motor vehicles. The emissions come from tail pipe exhausts, refueling of vehicles, and fuel evaporation. One way to cut back on these emissions would be to sharply reduce the number of cars and trucks in urban centers. Indeed, some cities restrict driving on days when air quality is poor. In addition, officials in major cities encourage motorists to use car pools with one car carrying five or six people rather than only the driver. In some metropolitan areas, special lanes on expressways are restricted to High Occupancy Vehicles (HOVs)—only those cars carrying three or more passengers. The special lanes reward car poolers with less congestion and faster travel time.

Still, many individuals do not want to give up their cars, regardless of the traffic congestion and dirty air. So more stringent measures might be needed. For example, New York City officials suggested charging motorists $10 per day to drive into the core city. But many theater, restaurant, and other business owners objected, saying the fee would keep customers away during the less-congested evening hours and hurt their businesses.

In the Los Angeles basin, which has recorded the highest ozone levels in the world, officials of the Air Quality Management District (AQMD) are trying to cut back on the millions of commuters on the road by requiring companies to reward employees who use car pools, buses, or bicycles to get to work. Companies that do not offer incentives will be fined $1,000 a day or more.[15]

Other measures include banning large diesel trucks from the highways during rush hours. In California, an estimated 850,000 diesel trucks and buses produce nearly as much nitrogen oxide as the total 8 million passenger vehicles in the state. California officials also are demanding stricter enforcement of laws that require motorists to install catalytic converters or to repair faulty ones on their vehicles. Auto manufacturers equip passenger vehicles with catalytic converters, which reduce tail pipe emissions of VOCs and nitrogen oxides, but some motorists have removed them illegally or have ruined their effectiveness by using leaded gasoline.

Another approach to controlling emissions from mobile sources is requiring automakers to install efficient charcoal-canister devices on vehicles. These devices, often called "onboard control systems," are designed to capture gas vapors during refueling. Vapors from the gas tank are collected in a carbon canister, then recycled into the engine where they are burned, thus preventing the release of hydrocarbons into the air.

Gas vapors can also be captured at the fuel pump. In some states, such as California, gas station owners must install vapor recovery devices on pump nozzles. These prevent the escape of VOC fumes when gas is pumped into vehicle tanks.

MAKING A CASE
FOR ALCOHOL FUELS

Alternative fuels such as methanol and ethanol are still another means of controlling VOCs. Although these fuels produce hydrocarbons, their hydrocarbons appear to be less reactive to photochemical processes than those of gasoline.

Methanol, known also as wood alcohol, is produced from natural gas or coal, and ethanol is distilled from corn. Both fuels can be added to petroleum or used as pure alcohol fuels. As additives, they provide more oxygen to gasoline fuel, which means that the mixture burns more cleanly and cuts carbon monoxide and ozone-producing emissions. Pure alcohol fuels

An ethanol plant sits surrounded by corn fields in northern Indiana. The plant processes corn to produce ethanol, a fuel that can be used in some cars as a substitute for a fossil fuel.

burn even cleaner than blends but create problems in vehicle engines that have rubber or plastic parts, which can be destroyed by alcohol. However, it is a relatively simple matter to produce alcohol-resistant parts for vehicles. Vehicles that successfully burn alcohol fuels have long been used in many South American countries.

Since 1979, the California Energy Commission (CEC) has worked with private industry to develop and test vehicles powered by alcohol fuels—an effort brought about first by oil shortages and then because of state legislation mandating cleaner-burning fuels. During 1980 and 1981, the state of California bought and used converted Ford and General Motors cars and trucks and Volkswagen Rabbits that would operate on ethanol and methanol. The state's energy commission also helped build an ethanol production plant, but it later concluded that "the production of ethanol as a transportation fuel in California was not cost effective."

Thus the CEC focused on methanol as a replacement for petroleum fuels, and fleets of several hundred cars and trucks have been operating on methanol fuel and have been driven hundreds of thousands of miles. The CEC found that methanol not only works well as a fuel in both light- and heavy-duty vehicles, but also offers pollution control benefits that bring the state closer to health standards set for ozone and nitrogen dioxide, as well as other air pollutants.

In 1987, the state of California contracted with Ford Motor Company to build 5,000 experimental vehicles, known by the generic term "fuel flexible vehicles," that will burn gasoline, methanol, or a blend of petroleum and alcohol fuels. At least 1,000 of these are in operation.

Another part of California's pollution control program is an air quality plan, adopted in January 1988,

To help combat air pollution, the state of California operates several model buses that use methanol fuel. Replacing diesel-powered buses with transit vehicles that operate on methanol can substantially reduce particulate and nitrogen oxide emissions.

that covers Los Angeles County and three other nearby counties. Within this area, all public agencies and private companies that operate fifteen or more vehicles will be required to switch from petroleum fuels to methanol by 1993. The plan would affect up to 400,000 vehicles, including 4,500 diesel-powered public buses, and would require building new gas stations or adapting existing stations to sell methanol fuel. The long-term goal is to replace at least 40 percent of the gas-powered passenger cars and 70 percent of the diesel-burning trucks operating in southern California. Overall, the state hopes to cut ozone pollution by 22 percent by the year 2000.

The use of ethanol as an alternative to petroleum fuels in the United States has taken a somewhat different twist. Ethanol was first used during the 1970s as an additive in gasoline, a blend known as gasohol, to extend fuel supplies when oil-producing nations in the Middle East cut production and caused gas shortages in the United States. Since the beginning of the 1980s, ethanol has replaced lead in some gasolines. Lead increases octane, or the ability of gas to resist engine knock, but it is toxic to humans who ingest it in fumes or other forms, so lead is being phased out of gasoline supplies. Ethanol is also an octane booster, but it apparently does not pose major health hazards.

In January 1988, Colorado's Air Quality Control Commission began an air pollution abatement program that requires the use of either ethanol (gasohol) or MTBE (methyl tertiary butyl ether), which is produced by chemical reactions of methanol and isobutylene. Since both fuels contain more oxygen atoms than standard gasolines, they are known as oxygenated, or "oxy," fuels.

The Colorado commission ordered that the oxy fuels be used during January and February along a heavily traveled corridor that includes Denver's metropolitan area and stretches from Fort Collins in the north to Colorado Springs in the south. Winter is the time when the area is plagued with inversions that trap not just ozone but carbon monoxide from motor vehicles as well as emissions from coal-burning power plants, refineries, and wood-burning stoves. So, along with regulations for oxy fuel use, there are also restrictions on wood burning and emissions from power plants and other sources of pollutants.

Although ethanol has been proven to significantly reduce carbon monoxide emissions, some EPA studies seem to indicate that it is less effective than methanol in reducing VOCs and might even increase VOC emissions. However, a recent study by Gary Whitten of Systems Application in San Raphael, California, took into account both the benefits and drawbacks of ethanol. Using computer models of the meteorology and the chemistry that leads to smog over seven California cities, Whitten found that in all seven cities the net effect of using ethanol blends was to reduce ozone. Follow-up studies using EPA's Urban Airshed Model, which provides a more thorough analysis of the same basic chemistry, will determine whether Whitten's conclusions are valid.[16]

CONTROVERSY OVER
CONTROL MEASURES

One of the difficulties in setting up pollution control measures is determining whether information provided by computer experts is accurate enough to use as a basis for regulations. Analysts apply mathematical formulas to create computer models that simulate polluted conditions over a given area. The models also suggest strategies for controlling air pollution. But some researchers doubt the results, believing there are too many unknowns, particularly in the complex chemistry of ozone pollution, to set up accurate control programs based on computer models.

Nevertheless, the EPA has developed two computer modeling programs that are considered highly reliable for predicting ozone transport. But because of the amount of time and personnel required to collect and validate data, and the computer capacity needed, these models are very costly to use. EPA officials say it costs from $300,000 to $500,000 to run the Urban Air-shed Model, for example. Costs for running an even more sophisticated Regional Oxidant Model are between $3 million and $5 million. The latter program has been used to effectively estimate the transport of air pollutants along the Northeast Corridor (from Maine to Virginia), but high operating costs have prevented widespread use for other areas of the nation.[17]

Another problem in applying controls is the matter of equity. For example, operators of some small businesses and industries that release relatively low amounts of VOCs believe they are being asked to bear an unfair economic burden. They insist that installing expensive control equipment would not make significant reductions in the ozone pollution problem. Larger companies, which have made efforts to control pollutants and are in areas that have almost reached compliance with the NAAQS, believe they should not have to add further controls when there are worse smog problems in other parts of the nation.

Business people say they do not want the federal government to make industries the scapegoat for ozone pollution problems. They believe there is too much emphasis on meeting ozone standards, arguing that those standards are met during most days of the year—about 98 percent to 99 percent of the time on a national scale. Before any new controls are put into effect, some business people insist that state regulatory agencies and federal EPA officials should improve ozone monitoring systems and get a more accurate inventory of sources that emit the precursors of ozone.

Still, many critics of the EPA's efforts to control ozone and other air pollutants have charged that the agency is too lax and does not aggressively enforce the Clean Air Act regulations. Critics point to the fact that for years the EPA has allowed some factories to increase emissions if owners can show they have reduced emissions elsewhere. But this practice of "equalizing" emissions is often abused.

The diversity of ozone-producing sources is one more major obstacle in meeting the national health standard for ozone. The EPA has set up basic guidelines for controlling ozone-producing emissions from stationary sources, and sometimes simple changes can be made to improve ambient air quality. For example, a spray-painting company might change its operation to use more efficient equipment and paints that are lower in VOCs.

In other instances a change requires new technology that takes years to develop. The Ohio Power Company, for example, spent more than a decade in research and millions of dollars to develop a clean-burning, coal-fired power plant. (Coal-burning often contributes to air pollution.) Construction began on the new plant in mid-1988. The first of its kind in the western hemisphere, the plant will burn coal under pressure on a bed of dolomite (a form of limestone) and will be able to "meet rigid air quality standards," a company bulletin stated. Ohio Power expects that its "clean coal technology" will be supplying electricity by the mid-1990s.

New technologies also are needed to control VOCs that come from wastewater and toxic waste treatment facilities. Individuals, too, need to be more aware that their daily activities contribute to air pollution problems. As EPA administrator J. Craig Potter explained: ". . . putting gas in your lawnmower, or painting your house with oil-based paint, or stripping a piece of furniture—those simple, everyday operations have the potential to create ozone because they involve the evaporation of volatile organic compounds into the air. But you have some substitutes. You can use water-based paint, for example."[18]

It is clear that controlling ozone depends on eliminating emissions of hydrocarbons and nitrogen oxides. But to do so, many citizens and government officials would have to take actions that would require changes in lifestyle that most of us resist. For example, most Americans do not want to give up their auto-based mode of transportation which steadily adds to not only pollution but also many other health-related problems, such as increased traffic accidents. A recent study by Worldwatch, a private research group, concluded that the U.S. government and other governments around the world need to encourage efforts to move away from an auto-centered society and to develop greater diversity in transportation, including expansion of public mass transit systems. But researchers, environmentalists, and government officials say that a vast public education program also must be initiated to inform people about the seriousness of air pollutants before any widespread pollution prevention programs can be effective.

ATTACKS ON THE OZONE SHIELD

Public education also plays a role in efforts to control pollutants that have been blamed for destroying parts of the ozone layer in the stratosphere. Until the 1970s, few people other than atmospheric scientists gave much thought to or were even aware of stratospheric ozone, let alone worried about what might be harming it.

Even in scientific circles, threats to the ozone layer were not a matter of major concern. Those scientists who had been studying ozone were more interested in theories about how the gas formed in the stratosphere and absorbed UV radiation. Another matter of interest was the discovery that ozone served as a marker or tracer, which helped scientists monitor changes in circulation patterns and the distribution of ozone in the atmosphere.

OZONE DISTRIBUTION

Although ozone makes up less than 1 ppm of all the gases in our planet's atmosphere, it is essential to life on earth. Scientists assume that in the early days of the earth's evolution there was no atmosphere, but gases from planet surfaces and volcanoes slowly collected. At first, the gases were little protection from the sun's UV radiation. But according to some evolutionary theories, life-forms on earth may have been able to develop in water that filtered out most of the UV rays but allowed enough visible light for chemical reactions to take place.

As organisms began to make use of the plentiful supply of oxygen on earth, the ozone layer also began to develop and to absorb most of the sun's UV rays that could harm crops, marine life, and human health. Both life on earth as we know it and the ozone layer that protects our planet's life support system depend on the oxygen supply in our atmosphere.

In the stratosphere, solar radiation breaks down molecular oxygen (O_2) into two oxygen atoms (O), which in turn combine with additional oxygen to form ozone (O_3), a process called photodissociation. Some of the ozone converts again to oxygen, and the process continues, creating a layer of ozone that surrounds the earth. The gaseous ozone not only absorbs UV radiation, but also determines stratospheric temperature and thus plays a role in the circulation patterns of the stratosphere.

According to Ralph J. Cicerone, a scientist at the National Center for Atmospheric Research (NCAR) in Boulder, Colorado, peak concentrations of ozone "are found between 25 and 35 km [16 and 22 miles]. The vertical column of O_3 is distributed roughly as follows: 0 to 10 km, 10%; 10 to 35 km, 80%; and above 35 km, 10%."[19] (A column of air is the amount of air along a vertical line starting from the ground and continuing up through the atmosphere.)

However, ozone concentrations are not static. Winds transport ozone throughout the stratosphere. Although ozone is constantly produced by the photo-chemical process, it is also destroyed by chemical reactions involving such gases as nitrogen, hydrogen, and chlorine. In addition, the amounts of ozone change with the seasons. The end result is that over centuries ozone in the stratosphere has maintained a dynamic equilibrium: the production and loss processes have balanced, keeping a layer of ozone around the planet that protects all life from too much UV radiation. However, that delicate balance now may be threatened, scientists say.

DISCOVERY OF THE OZONE "HOLE"

Why did scientists become concerned about the ozone layer? A number of events prompted scientific research into the possibility that the ozone layer might be in danger. One was a debate that developed over a fleet of several hundred huge aircraft, called supersonic trans-ports (SSTs). Congress planned to fund the manufac-ture of two U.S. prototype SSTs, modeled after the Concorde built in France, and congressional leaders wanted information on what impact the SSTs would have on the stratosphere where the aircraft would be flying. Scientific studies during the early 1970s showed that SSTs flying through the stratosphere released ni-trogen oxides in exhaust gases. Ironically, nitrogen compounds that help produce ozone in the troposphere are part of a chemical process that destroys ozone in the stratosphere. Although the threat to the ozone layer was a consideration in whether or not SSTs should be manufactured, the project eventually was dropped be-cause the production of SSTs became too costly.

About the same time that the SST debate was going on, teams of scientists at the University of Michi-

gan, Harvard, and the Palo Alto (California) Research
Center were investigating the effects of the space shuttle on the environment. Researchers found that exhausts from the space shuttle's engines released
chlorine species into the atmosphere, but at first little
was known about how chlorine compounds affected the
stratosphere. As research continued, studies suggested that sixty shuttle launches a year would release
only enough chemically active chlorine to reduce ozone
concentrations by 0.2 percent. Nevertheless, the research on the stratospheric effects of shuttle launches
alerted others in the scientific community and in government agencies to view chlorine compounds as possible threats to the ozone layer.[20]

Even before the research into environmental im-
pacts of the SST and the space shuttle, a British chemist, James Lovelock, had invented an instrument that
could detect chlorofluorocarbons (CFCs), gases con-
sisting of chlorine, fluorine, and carbon that are produced by a variety of human activities and released into
the atmosphere from many sources. Lovelock wanted
to know what was happening to these chemicals after
they were emitted. He found traces of CFCs in remote
areas far from their major sources, and theorized that
CFCs stayed in the atmosphere and might have an
impact on atmospheric chemistry.

Then, in 1974, F. Sherwood Rowland and Mario J.
Molina, both in the chemistry department of the University of California at Irvine, released a study proposing
that CFCs percolated through the troposphere into the
stratosphere, altering the chemistry of the protective
ozone layer. That proposal sounded an alarm. Atmospheric scientists in many nations followed up with
studies that confirmed the findings of Rowland and Molina. At the same time, the possible threat to the ozone
layer caught the attention of the general public.

Since CFCs were used in aerosol sprays for hundreds of different kinds of consumer products, worried consumers, environmentalists, and other groups called for bans on CFCs in aerosol sprays. In 1978, the U.S. Congress passed legislation that outlawed the manufacture of CFC aerosols. Canadian, Swiss, and Scandinavian governments took similar actions. However, CFCs still are used widely in aerosol products manufactured in other nations and in a variety of U.S. products, including refrigerators, air conditioners, and foam packaging, and in solvents for cleaning computer circuit boards.

It is not surprising that industrial users for many years have fought a total ban on CFCs. When the gases were first developed by chemists at General Motors Corporation in the early 1930s, they were thought to be almost perfect chemicals because they are stable and do not react easily with other substances. In fact, CFCs replaced toxic and flammable gases once used as coolants in refrigerators. Since CFCs are nonflammable, nontoxic, and noncorrosive, they can be used in a variety of products without the worry of drastic changes in their properties or the threat of fire and other hazards. But the great stability of CFCs also allows them to survive for many years and "pile up" in the troposphere. As a result, some CFCs eventually move into the stratosphere, where they can destroy ozone.

Recently, public attention again has focused on the damaging effects of CFCs on the ozone layer. In 1985, British atmospheric scientists, who operated an observation station at Halley Bay on the coast of Antarctica, published a startling report: concentrations of ozone over Antarctica had been dropping, but just during September and October, the austral (southern hemisphere) spring. Only during this season did there appear to be a thinning of the protective ozone layer.

The scientists, who were with the British Antarctic Survey team, had been collecting data for decades. They found that almost half of the vertical column of ozone over the South Pole failed to appear every season. The phenomenon, which later was dubbed a "hole," occurred repeatedly, with increasing amounts of ozone loss each season between 1977 and 1984.

Why did the British scientists wait so long to report their findings? One reason was because the British thought their observations were in error. At first their findings did not seem to be supported by readings from U.S. satellite instruments measuring ozone levels. But the British checked measurements at another station on the Argentine Islands, about 1,000 miles (1,600 km) to the northwest. Similar ozone losses had been recorded there.

In the meantime, after the British published their findings, the National Aeronautics and Space Administration (NASA), the National Oceanic and Atmospheric Administration (NOAA), and other U.S. facilities quickly reviewed ozone data they had been collecting since the mid-1970s. They found that NASA satellites had recorded seasonal drops in ozone over Antarctica, but the computer program used to read the data had been designed to reject major decreases or increases in ozone levels as "improbable." Thus U.S. reviewers concluded that their data supported the British findings. The ozone "hole" was very real—the size of the continental United States—and computer models of stratospheric chemistry and dynamics (circulation patterns) had not been able to predict such a major depletion of Antarctic ozone.

OZONE DEPLETION THEORIES

To back up their reviews, leading U.S. atmospheric scientists and engineers formed an interagency team to step up ozone research. American researchers, along with scientists from other nations, have taken part in several expeditions to the Antarctic region since late 1986. During their expeditions, researchers not only confirmed the data showing a much greater depletion of ozone over the South Pole during austral spring than had been predicted previously, but they also collected more data to help explain the causes of the ozone depletion.

Although the most widely accepted theory links ozone loss to chemical reactions involving CFCs in the stratosphere, two other distinct theories on causes of the ozone "hole" have been proposed. One centers on enhanced solar activity during sunspot cycles. Over a period of approximately eleven years, the number of visible sunspots, caused by magnetic activity on the sun, increases to a maximum and then decreases. This sunspot cycle brings with it increased solar activity, such as a spectacular discharge of energy called a flare.

With intense solar activity, such as the period from late 1979 to early 1980, more UV radiation reaches the earth. Thus, according to the solar-cycle theory, the production of naturally occurring nitrogen compounds increased in the mesosphere and lower thermosphere (layers of atmosphere above the stratosphere). During the polar night (the winter months when there is no sun), nitrogen compounds moved downward and with the arrival of spring sunlight reacted to deplete ozone in the lower and middle stratosphere. The assumption is that stratospheric ozone over Antarctica eventually will be replenished with the decrease in solar activity.

Most atmospheric scientists reject the solar-cycle theory, however, arguing that supporting evidence is weak. According to the theory, there should be "significant losses [of ozone] well above 20 kilometers

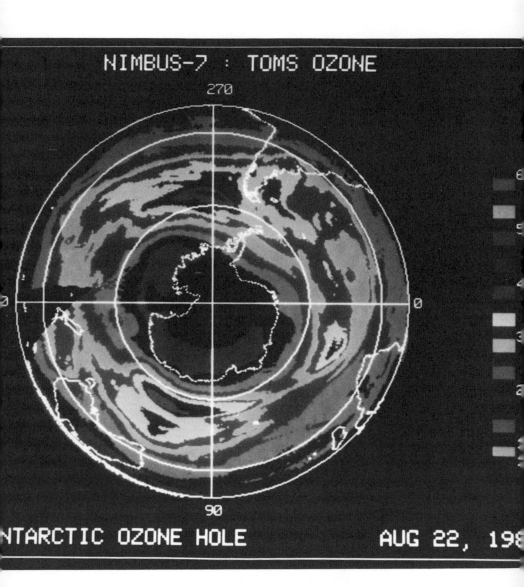

The Antarctic Ozone Hole is shown in this picture produced by NASA using data from the Nimbus 7 Total Ozone Mapping Spectrometer (TOMS) instrument which monitors the ozone over the entire Earth. The ozone "hole" is the oval feature covering the Antarctic.

[12 mi]."[21] But members of the Antarctic expeditions point out that ozone loss is about 12 to 22 kilometers (7 to 14 mi). Scientists at Antarctica also found that nitrogen monoxide and nitrogen dioxide concentrations within the hole were the lowest measured anywhere. If the solar-cycle theory were correct, large amounts of those gases should appear in ozone-depleted air.

Another major theory for stratospheric ozone loss stresses changing climate and dynamics. Basically, dynamicists believe that winds redistribute ozone, and changing climate and circulation patterns largely determine the amount of ozone in a region.

To explain circulation patterns, one scientist pointed out in a *Scientific American* report that air in the stratosphere circulates "from high altitudes in the Tropics toward lower altitudes in the polar regions, carrying newly made ozone with it. In the Northern Hemisphere stratospheric air circulates all the way to the North Pole" where ozone levels are high, but circulation in the Southern Hemisphere "goes only as far as about 60 degrees south latitude for most of the year."[22]

According to the dynamic theory, the climate and wind patterns of the Antarctic prevent ozone-rich air from moving farther south until late November or early December (late spring or early summer of the austral seasons). The Antarctic is surrounded by a belt of swirling winds, an isolated air mass called the polar vortex. The vortex begins to break up in late spring, and an influx of air with higher ozone concentrations can then "fill in" the hole over the Antarctic.

Some dynamicists believe that a "type of upwelling may also be responsible for the seasonal formation of the Antarctic ozone hole. When the sun begins to shine on the stratosphere after it has been cooled during the dark polar winter, the air is rapidly heated. Because the suddenly warmed air is unable to dissipate all of its heat through radiation, it rises ... the upwelling air moves ozone out of the lower stratosphere above Antarctica and brings it to midlatitudes," one report theorized.[23]

Since 1986, a number of expeditions to the South Pole have provided strong evidence to support the theory that chlorine compounds are responsible for much of the ozone loss over Antarctica. There was debate over how chlorine compounds destroy ozone, but most atmospheric chemists now theorize that chlorine monoxide from human-produced CFCs accumulate in the stratosphere. Reactive chlorine then comes in contact with clouds of microscopic ice particles formed from water vapor and chemical compounds. These polar stratospheric clouds (PSCs), as they are called, provide a surface for the catalytic process (chemical reactions) to take place when the sun appears over Antarctica in early September. Basically, chlorine nitrate and hydrogen chloride, which are relatively inert, are converted to active chlorine compounds that can attack ozone.

Atmospheric chemist F. Sherwood Rowland, who first presented the idea that chlorine destroys ozone, has noted that each free chlorine atom can destroy 100,000 molecules of ozone before its chain reaction has been completed. Elevated amounts of chlorine dioxide, a by-product of the chemical reaction, and chlorine monoxide, which actually destroys ozone, are considered signs that CFCs are responsible for stratospheric ozone loss. Other chemicals may also be involved in the reactions that take place in the stratosphere, and research is continuing on the chemistry of PSCs.

However, the chemical theory does not discount the concept that solar-cycle activity creates short-term changes in ozone levels and that meteorology plays an important role in the formation of the ozone "hole."

Daniel L. Albritton, director of NOAA's Aeronomy Laboratory in Boulder, Colorado, where scientists study the chemistry and dynamics of the atmosphere, explained this theory in testimony before the U.S. Senate Committee on Environment and Public Works, noting that

> the current picture of the "ozone hole" is one of an exquisite balance of meteorology and chemistry. Specifically, the unusual physical conditions in Antarctica play a key role in the case of the "ozone hole." Namely, the low temperatures cause ice particles to form. The ice particles do two things. First their surfaces host reactions that convert chlorine from the non-reactive form to the reactive form. Secondly, as they grow, the ice particles remove reactive nitrogen from the Antarctic stratosphere, which is a chemical change that permits the chlorine to stay in the reactive form, rather than convert back to the non-reactive form. Lastly, ... [there are] persistent and elevated abundances of reactive chlorine monoxide [that] destroy ozone. . . .[24]

THE NATURE OF
THE CULPRITS

Of the large amounts of chlorine compounds that have been found in the Antarctic ozone hole, some chlorine comes from such natural sources as the oceans. But, according to a NOAA report, four times more chlorine comes from a type of human-produced hydrocarbons that include the CFCs already described. In this class of hydrocarbons, hydrogen atoms have been replaced by a halogen—chlorine (Cl), bromine (Br), or fluorine (F) atom. When some of the hydrogen atoms are replaced by a halogen, the resulting compound is known as a partially halogened compound; when all of the hydrogen atoms are replaced by halogens, the compound is fully halogenated.[25]

Several factors determine whether the halogenated hydrocarbons, called halogens or halocarbons, will deplete ozone. The first is the release rate of the chemical compound into the atmosphere. A second factor is the rate at which the compound moves up from the troposphere into the stratosphere. A third is the amount of time it takes for compounds to go through the photochemical process in the stratosphere. Finally, ozone loss depends on how well halogen fragments destroy ozone.

Using the properties of chemical compounds, scientists estimate the ozone depleting potential (ODP) of halogens. One variety of fully halogenated hydrocarbons are the CFCs, known by such names as CFC 11, CFC 12, and CFC 113, which are "the largest contributors . . . to the predicted depletion of ozone," according to the NOAA report.

Halogenated bromine compounds, called halons, are even more effective in destroying ozone. For example, a molecule of the compound halon 1301 (the compound used in fire extinguishers) is ten times more effective in destroying ozone than a molecule of the compound CFC 11, a gas used in refrigeration and the manufacture of foam products.

Overall, much smaller amounts of halons than CFCs are used, but worldwide a total of many hundreds of millions of kilograms of halons and CFCs are produced each year. Some of the compounds that have the highest ODPs have a lifetime of well over one hundred years in the troposphere.

A fire extinguisher containing halon 1211 is the type used to put out fires in art museums, rare book libraries, computer rooms, and other areas with sensitive equipment. Halon 1211 does not destroy priceless collections or expensive equipment, but it contributes to stratospheric ozone depletion.

GLOBAL OZONE LOSSES

Because of their long lifetimes, CFCs and halons are expected to increase in the stratosphere even if emissions of these compounds stay the same or drop in the next few decades. In other words, the compounds have been accumulating and move slowly from the troposphere into the stratosphere.

How will an increase in halogens affect the stratospheric ozone worldwide? The balance of global ozone
depends on a variety of factors, including meteorology,
chemical reactions, and the presence of other trace
gases. Although there have been suggestions that
global ozone losses might correspond to the increase of
chlorine emissions, scientists have found no direct evidence that the chemistry of total ozone worldwide is the
same as the Antarctic ozone during the polar spring.
For example, very cold temperatures and PSCs that set
the stage for chlorine reactions are not present in
warmer climates. But there have been speculations that
sulfur gases might provide surfaces for ozone-depleting
reactions to take place in the stratosphere.

Many questions about depletion of the ozone layer
are still unanswered. Since the early 1980s, scientists in
the United States and in other nations have made great
progress in efforts to understand the chemistry and
distribution of stratospheric ozone. Much of that progress has depended on research expeditions to measure
ozone in the stratosphere over the South and North
Poles.

TAKING
MEASUREMENTS

After the British discovery of the ozone "hole," U.S. researchers reviewed data from Dobson spectrophotometers—ground-based instruments that have been used at various sites since the 1950s to measure ozone distribution on a global scale. The Dobson instrument, named for the British scientist who developed it, measures UV radiation, which strikes the surface of the earth at various wavelengths as the angle of the sun changes.

Since ozone absorbs radiation at different wavelengths, that measurement can be compared to the amount coming from the sun. Ozone levels are expressed in Dobson units, or hundredths of a millimeter. (One hundred Dobson units equals four hundredths of an inch of pure ozone at the earth's surface.) For example, the ozone levels in the Antarctic "hole" varied in 1986 from a low of less than 200 Dobson units to over 400 Dobson units—the standard concentration before the ozone began to thin.

The researchers also reviewed data from satellite instruments used to measure the levels of stratospheric ozone. The Total Ozone Mapping Spectrometer (TOMS) and a companion instrument called the Solar Backscatter Ultraviolet (SBUV) instrument aboard the *Nimbus 7* satellite have provided daily maps of total column ozone since the late 1970s. But diffuser plates that reflect solar radiation into the instruments have degraded over time. In order to get a "normalized" measurement, the satellite measurements were compared to those of the ground-based Dobson instruments. Scientists also took into account natural phenomena that could affect the ozone level, such as volcanic eruptions, the solar sunspot cycle, and changes in stratospheric winds. Analysis of the data confirmed the global decrease in ozone levels as well as the seasonal Antarctic "hole" in the ozone layer.

Nevertheless, the ozone science community knew that much more information was needed, and U.S. scientists planned a ground-based expedition to McMurdo Station, a National Science Foundation (NSF) research site in Antarctica. U.S. agencies (NSF, NASA, and NOAA) and the Chemical Manufacturer's Association (CMA) provided financial backing and also the personnel needed to accurately observe and record data.

THE 1986 NATIONAL OZONE EXPEDITION

Susan Solomon, an atmospheric chemist working at NOAA's Aeronomy Laboratory in Boulder, Colorado, was chosen to lead the 1986 National Ozone Expedition, now dubbed NOZE I.

With the use of sophisticated computer models, Solomon, along with many other scientists, had been developing for several years theories about the chemistry in the stratosphere. In a number of published scientific papers, some written in collaboration with colleagues at NCAR, Solomon had suggested that the thinning of the ozone layer over Antarctica was due to chemical reactions brought on by human-produced chlorine compounds in association with the clouds and the dry, frigid conditions over the South Pole. Her theoretical work provided a broad background for overseeing the expedition.

Plans for the expedition got underway in early 1986. The research team of seventeen had to be ready to go to Antarctica during late August, just before austral spring. As Solomon explained it: "Antarctica can only be accessed at certain times of the year—the [McMurdo] station is only open from October to February, although every year a few planes carrying work crews are sent in during late August. The crews prepare the runway, making a smooth ice surface to allow wheeled aircraft to land; earlier in the year the runway area is covered with snow, and planes would have to land on skis."

To get to the Antarctic, the expedition team flew first to New Zealand. From there, a Navy pilot flew the team to the polar site, a nine-hour trip over water. Since there are not many daylight hours during late winter in Antarctica, the pilot informed the research team that they would leave at 3:00 A.M. With arrival time expected to be around noon, there would be some light in case an emergency landing became necessary.

Solomon, who has made subsequent journeys to the polar regions, admitted that preparing for the first flight was "a bit unnerving. Before takeoff, the pilot announced that we would reach a PSR (point of safe return)—halfway across. Beyond that point, we could not turn back; there would only be enough fuel to reach the observation station."[26]

After landing without incident, the expedition members began to set up their observation instruments, which they would use over the next two months to gather data about the stratosphere. One of the instruments was a visible light spectrometer that measures visible wavelengths, or series of color bands, from light sources—the sun and the moon. Since various chemicals in the stratosphere absorb different wavelengths or colors, the instrument could measure the amount of such compounds as chlorine dioxide and nitrogen dioxide in the thinning ozone layer of Antarctica. Data showed that there were exceedingly low levels of nitrogen dioxide that inhibit ozone loss when it "ties up" active chlorine; there were also large amounts of highly reactive chlorine compounds believed responsible for ozone depletion. In fact, as Solomon put it: "The 1986 measurements showed that chlorine dioxide levels were fifty times greater than what had been expected, and chlorine monoxide was one hundred times greater than expected levels."

During the 1986 expedition, scientists also launched high-altitude balloons with ozonesonde instruments, which use electrochemical sensors to measure ozone. The balloons could travel into the stratosphere and beam findings from sensors back to instruments being read by specialists at the observation station. From August 25 to November 6, 1986, re-

*Jim Carpenter, member of
the University of Wyoming,
Laramie research team,
prepares to launch a balloon
with instruments that will
measure stratospheric ozone.*

searchers made thirty-three balloon launches, confirming not only some of the findings from the spectrometer observations, but also the altitude of the Antarctic ozone "hole"—from about 12 to 22 kilometers (7 to 14 mi).

1987 EXPEDITIONS

Although all of the 1986 Antarctic experiments provided important data on the chemistry of the stratosphere over the South Pole, there were still many questions regarding the causes of ozone loss. To further test the theory that chemicals from human activities are partly responsible for the ozone "hole" and to learn more about the role of meteorology in ozone loss, researchers set up more data-gathering expeditions for the summer of 1987. NASA coordinated the $10 million campaign, which was sponsored by nineteen U.S. and international agencies.

Called the Airborne Antarctic Ozone Experiment, it involved 150 scientists and technicians from four nations who were linked by an international telecommunications network—via satellite and computers—to other researchers at participating agencies. The researchers also received nearly on-the-spot (real-time) observations from satellite instruments. The satellite observations helped pilots develop daily flight plans for NASA research planes that were flown a total of twenty-five missions over Antarctica from a base in Punta Arenas, Chile, the southernmost city in the world.

The aircraft—one a DC-8, a former passenger plane set up like a laboratory, and the other a modified spy plane called an ER-2—were equipped to probe the stratosphere with a variety of instruments. Although the DC-8 usually flies below the stratosphere, scientists on board used laser radar instruments to monitor the Antarctic ozone "hole." One, called the Differential Absorption Lidar (DIAL) system, beamed four wavelengths of light through an observation window on the roof of the DC-8. The DIAL system provided research scientists with color plots showing the distribution of ozone and PSC cloud formations.

Research scientists on the DC-8 also analyzed air samples, drawing outside air into an instrument called a

A NASA pilot boards the ER-2 cockpit during the 1987 Airborne Antarctic Ozone Experiment. The ER-2 is equipped with fourteen instruments designed to probe the stratosphere.

chemiluminescent ozone detector, which observes the chemical reaction between ozone and ethylene and records the concentration of ozone. The instrument is so sensitive that in a billion parts of air only two parts per billion (ppb) of ozone would be detected.

According to NASA, the ER-2 was able to fly "at altitudes ranging from 12 to 18 kilometers [7 to 11 mi] above the Earth's surface, well into the altitude region where ozone is undergoing depletion." Instruments on the ER-2 measured distributions of ozone, chlorine and nitrogen compounds, and the makeup of ice crystals in the stratosphere.

While the aircraft missions were underway, satellite instruments provided daily measurements of the extent of the ozone "hole." Researchers at four ground locations, including McMurdo, launched balloon ozonesonde instruments, recording measurements to add to the long-term data on ozone loss. In addition, a second ground-based NOZE expedition returned to McMurdo. According to team leader Solomon, NOZE II findings strengthened the theory that cloud formations provide the surfaces needed for ozone-destroying chemical reactions to take place.

THE OZONE TRENDS PANEL

While various polar expeditions were underway in 1986 and 1987, atmospheric scientists also were continuing their comprehensive study of the reports, computer modeling, satellite observations, and other data gathered on ozone depletion. This study group, called the Ozone Trends Panel (OTP), formed in October 1986, primarily in response to the earlier reports on the Antarctic and global-scale decreases in ozone. Under the direction of NASA and in collaboration with NOAA, the Federal Aviation Administration (FAA), the World Meteorological Organization (WMO), and the United Nations Environment Program (UNEP), the panel included more than one hundred scientists from the United States and many other nations.

In March 1988, after sixteen months of study, the OTP released a report from NASA headquarters in Washington, D.C. According to Robert Watson, NASA scientist and chairman of the panel, there appeared to be little doubt that human-produced chlorofluorocarbons "are primarily responsible for the observed decrease in ozone within the polar vortex [Antarctic region]."

The panel confirmed that "there has been a large, sudden, and unexpected decrease in the abundance of springtime Antarctic ozone over the last decade. Ozone decreases of more than 50 percent in the total column, and 95 percent locally between 15 and 20 kilometers [9 and 12 mi] altitude have been observed. The total column of ozone in the austral spring of 1987 at all latitudes south of 60 degrees south was the lowest since measurements began 30 years ago . . . The unique meteorology during winter and spring over Antarctica sets up the special conditions" for ozone depletion, the panel noted.[27]

In addition, the panel found that the ozone layer worldwide is thinning. Although the levels of ozone fluctuate, global stratospheric ozone has decreased an average of 2.5 percent from the mid-1970s to the mid-1980s. The greatest ozone losses have been in the Tropics, but ozone losses also have been recorded over the United States, Europe, China, Japan, and part of the Soviet Union.

In their report, panel members were careful to point out that policy makers in government and the general public should not be surprised if ozone levels increase for a time. Increasing solar activity until 1991 may reverse the decrease in ozone. However, the panel reported that "after 1991, when the solar ultraviolet output begins to decline, the total column ozone is again predicted to decrease."[28]

CURRENT RESEARCH

Global destruction of ozone could create serious problems for the environment and human health. Loss of global ozone could change climate patterns as well, although scientists are not sure where and how those changes would take place. Thus scientists have continued to study the chemistry of the stratosphere in a NOZE III expedition to Antarctica. Researchers also are stepping up the pace of ozone observations over the North Pole.

Western scientists have been monitoring the Arctic region from four stations—one each in Alaska and Canada, and two in Norway. Norwegian scientists noted an ozone deficit over the Arctic in mid-1986, but the thinning appeared minor and was only transitory. Then in February 1988, a team of U.S. atmospheric scientists went to Thule, Greenland to study the chemistry of the stratosphere over the North Pole.

In May 1988, the scientific team reported its findings: Large amounts of chlorine dioxide had been detected over the Arctic and climatic conditions were similar to that of the Antarctic—a swirling vortex, cold temperatures, and stratospheric clouds that contribute to the ozone-destroying process. The researchers also found much lower levels of nitrogen dioxide than would be present in the "standard" chemistry of the atmosphere in which there is enough nitrogen dioxide to convert active chlorine compounds into nonreactive forms. Thus all the factors put together strongly suggested that "the same thing that is going on in Antarctica is also happening in the Arctic for a few months," one of the researchers told a *Science News* reporter.[29]

Further study of the North Pole region continued in January 1989 with ground-based research and an airborne expedition similar to the campaign from Punta Arenas, Chile. Based in Stavanger, Norway, scientists, who spent six weeks gathering data, reported finding high levels of chlorine gases and PSCs, but no evidence of significant ozone losses. However, they expressed concern that atmospheric conditions over the Arctic coupled with increasing pollution could lead to depletion of ozone over the North Pole.

EFFECTS OF STRATOSPHERIC OZONE LOSS

Since stratospheric ozone protects life on earth, the loss of ozone suggests the possibility that plants, animals, and people are in grave danger. Certainly, if all ozone were destroyed, UV radiation from the sun could "zap" us all. For the moment, though, the earth is not threatened with utter destruction. Fluctuations in global ozone and depletion of ozone over the polar regions produce more subtle, albeit grim, effects.

In June 1986, dozens of detailed, scientific reports on the effects of ozone loss and climate change were presented to over three hundred participants of an international conference sponsored by the United Nations Environment Program (UNEP) and the U.S. EPA. Scientists, government officials, representatives from industries and environmental groups from about twenty countries took part in the four-day event.

One of a series of environmental conferences, the summer 1986 gathering had been preceded by three other major international meetings in less than a year to discuss the nature of ozone depletion and climate change problems. Through discussions and publication of scientific papers, conference members hoped to improve the world's understanding of how atmospheric changes can affect life systems on a global scale. Proceedings of the June 1986 conference filled four volumes, which were published by the EPA. Still, as the introduction to Volume 1 noted, the published papers "barely scratched the surface in discovering and demonstrating the possible risks of ozone modification and climate change. A continual evolution of our understanding will be necessary for our knowledge to stay ahead of the global experiment [on the earth's atmosphere] that society is conducting."[30]

HUMAN HEALTH PROBLEMS

According to research reports at the June 1986 international conference and other published reports since that time, a one percent loss in stratospheric ozone results in a two percent increase in UV radiation. In turn, the increased radiation could cause a variety of human health problems, including damage to the immune system, which would weaken the body's ability to fight diseases, and higher incidences of such eye disorders as cataracts, retinal damage, and corneal tumors.

Increased UV radiation also would bring about more cases of skin problems such as premature aging of the skin and higher incidences of squamous-cell carcinoma, a type of nonmalignant cancer that affects mostly light-skinned people.

Researcher Edward A. Emmett of Johns Hopkins Medical School in Baltimore, Maryland, has noted that controlled studies show the characteristics which put people at risk for skin cancer. These risk factors "include fair complexion, light eye color, light original hair

color, poor ability to tan, and easy and repeated sunburns. Persons of Celtic (Scottish, Irish, Welsh) descent
may be particularly vulnerable," even if they do not
exactly fit the risk profile, Emmett reported.[31] Dark-
skinned people are relatively safe from nonmalignant
skin cancer because the melanin pigment in the skin
provides protection from UV damage.

Currently, more than 500,000 Americans each
year develop skin cancer. With each one percent loss in
ozone, the skin cancer rate is expected to increase by
three to six percent. Although the vast majority of skin
cancers can be cured, one type, melanoma, is more
dangerous and affects people of all skin colors. An
estimated 6,000 Americans died from the disease in
1988, and the number of cases is expected to rise. In
some instances melanoma has been linked to blistering
sunburns, but the disease is more likely related to ge-
netic factors, viruses, and exposure to chemical car-
cinogens (cancer-causing substances).

The American Cancer Society, the Skin Cancer
Foundation, dermatologists, and other medical experts
urge people to take protective measures such as the
following to prevent nonmalignant skin cancer:

• wear wide-brimmed hats and clothing that covers the skin when exposed to the sun for long periods.

• avoid the use of sun reflectors.

• watch out for cloudy or overcast days when UV
rays may still burn.

• limit "sunbathing" time to before 10:00 A.M. and
after 3:00 P.M.

• use sunscreen lotions or sunblocks that can
screen out harmful UV rays; for people with light and
sensitive skin, most dermatologists recommend sunblocks with a sun-protection factor (SPF) of 15.

Increased UV radiation, which is the result of ozone loss in the stratosphere, can lead to a variety of skin diseases unless people use protective measures such as applying sunscreen lotions or limiting their time under the sun's rays.

Because of greater public awareness of the harmful effects of UV radiation, many more people are buying sunscreens, which have SPFs greater than 15. Sunscreen products are rated according to the amount of time a person with a certain skin type can be exposed to the sun without burning. A sunscreen with an SPF of 6, for example, allows a person to be exposed to the sun six times longer than someone who does not use a protective lotion or cream.

According to recent news reports, the products with SPFs in the twenties and thirties are being marketed as "ultra-sunscreens" and are touted as lotions that allow sunbathers to spend more time in the sun without burning. However, the reports point out that "many dermatologists are skeptical" and believe that a product with an SPF of 15 if used properly is protection enough. The Food and Drug Administration (FDA) is trying to determine whether the "ultra-sunscreens" are as they claim. There is also concern that the high concentrations of chemicals in the sunblocks can be toxic, *Newsweek* reported.[32]

Regardless of the measures taken to lower one's risk of skin cancer, there is always the possibility that it will be increasingly difficult to guard against health hazards posed by additional ozone depletion. Scientists are just beginning to learn how people can protect themselves living under a depleted ozone layer. For example, monitoring programs are underway at U.S. research stations in the Antarctic regions to try to determine the extent of dangers to working crews exposed to UV radiation. Peter Wilkniss of the U.S. National Science Foundation believes that crews, who spend months in darkness during the Antarctic winter, may be highly susceptible to UV radiation when spring arrives. Living in darkness for six to eight months can affect a person's immune and hormonal systems, which in turn may create a greater risk of developing eye and skin disorders when exposed to sunlight and greater ozone depletion.[33]

ENVIRONMENTAL EFFECTS

Since the 1970s, a number of experiments have been conducted at research universities to determine how UV radiation affects land-based plants and marine life.

According to a research report presented at the June 1986 international conference and summarized by the World Resources Institute (WRI), enhanced UV radiation could slow the process of photosynthesis, reduce leaf area, and decrease water use efficiency in many plants.[34] Thus yields of some crops such as soybeans would decrease, costing billions of dollars in crop losses.

Aquatic life also could be endangered by ozone depletion. Although some aquatic species such as anchovy larvae have developed a tolerance for increased UV radiation, greater ozone depletion might result in abnormal development of larvae or kill of larvae, which are used worldwide in animal feeds. There is some speculation that organisms such as blue-green algae that are unharmed by UV light could dominate aquatic systems.

Carl Sagan, a professor of astronomy and space sciences at Cornell, who has written many articles and books on environmental subjects, summed it up this way in a *Parade* magazine article:

> If increasing u.v. falls on the oceans, the damage is not restricted to ... little plants— because they are the food of one-celled animals, who are eaten in turn by little shrimplike crustaceans, who are eaten by small fish, who are eaten by large fish, who are eaten by dolphins, whales and people. The destruction of the little plants at the basis of the food chain causes the entire chain to collapse. There are many such food chains, on land as in water, and all of them seem vulnerable to disruption by u.v. For example, the bacteria in the roots of rice plants that grab nitrogen from the air are u.v.-sensitive.

Increasing u.v. may threaten crops and pos-
sibly even compromise the human food
supply.[35]

Other direct effects of increased UV radiation include
damages to various polyvinyl, or plastic, materials used
in construction. UV radiation discolors rigid vinyl home
siding, for example, and also may cause vinyl pipelines
to become brittle, leading to even more serious problems if, say, natural gas pipes should leak or burst.

Indirectly, added UV radiation is expected to stimu-
late climatic conditions that promote smog—ozone pollution. Studies show that "ozone concentrations would
peak earlier in the day and at greater distances from the
source, with the result that a larger human population
would be exposed and at risk."[36]

LINKS TO THE
"GREENHOUSE EFFECT"

Gases that help destroy stratospheric ozone also play a
part in another environmental problem: the gradual
warming of the earth due to an enhanced greenhouse
effect. In the natural scheme of things, the greenhouse
effect is a process by which the sun's infrared rays hit
the earth's surface and then radiate heat back into the
troposphere.

Some heat escapes into space but the rest is
trapped by naturally occurring carbon dioxide and other
gases that act somewhat like the glass of a greenhouse
surrounding the earth, keeping it warm. Without the
warming, the planet would be too cold to sustain life. But
human activities have loaded the atmosphere with carbon dioxide, CFCs, and such gases as methane and
nitrous oxide, creating an imbalance in the climate system—an enhanced or forced greenhouse effect, which

scientists predict could, by the middle of the next century, make the earth warmer than it has been in the last two million years.[37]

The increased concentration of carbon dioxide comes from industries and power plants that burn fossil fuels (oil, coal, and natural gas) and emit gaseous compounds from smokestacks. Additional carbon dioxide comes from vast forests, particularly the Amazon forests in Brazil, that have been cleared to provide cropland or cut for the lumber. Trees "hold" carbon dioxide during the process of photosynthesis, but when deforestation takes place, carbon dioxide is released into the atmosphere.

Increases in other greenhouse gases also are linked to human activities. Nitrous oxide, for example, is a greenhouse gas that comes from chemical fertilizers and emissions from motor vehicles.

Another greenhouse gas is methane, which comes from cattle waste, termite nests, and rice paddies. In 1987, atmospheric chemists at the University of California in Irvine released a report showing that methane had steadily increased in the troposphere and measured 1.7 ppm, 11 percent higher than a decade before and 2.4 times higher than it has been over the past 160,000 years.

Atmospheric scientists are looking at the possibility that increased cattle raising, increases in the amount of acreage worldwide devoted to rice planting, and an explosion of termite populations which thrive in areas where vast tropical forests have been burned away may account for some of the rise in methane levels. But no one is certain what all the methane sources are or how much the gas contributes to global warming, although its effect is probably much greater than once thought.[38]

As greenhouse gases build up in the atmosphere,

they contribute to a heat trap that is pushing the earth's average temperature up between one and two degrees Celsius (1.8 to 3.6 degrees Fahrenheit), according to an October 1988 report from the U.S. EPA. To people in cold climates, the temperature rise does not appear significant, but in some areas the temperature may rise as much as eight or nine degrees and the "ripple effect" of climate changes can be disastrous.

Atmospheric scientists continue to express concerns about weather and environmental changes that would occur as the result of increased warming. The researchers repeatedly have predicted that global warming would cause some polar ice to melt, thus raising the levels of oceans and flooding coastal cities like New York and such countries as the Netherlands and Bangladesh.

Rainfall patterns are expected to change also, with more droughts in the midsection of the United States and more precipitation in Canada, the Soviet Union, and Scandinavia, increasing growing seasons in those areas. Award-winning scientist Bert Bolin of the World Meteorological Organization believes the greenhouse warming of the earth is a problem that "is 10 times or maybe 100 times more important and more difficult" than stratospheric ozone losses. However, Bolin was not suggesting that depletion of the ozone layer should be ignored—the two problems, as many scientists have pointed out, are interrelated.

Another expert on the greenhouse effect, James E. Hansen, director of NASA's Goddard Institute for Space Studies in New York, has said in recent U.S. Senate hearings and in media interviews that he is "99 percent certain" that climate changes due to an enhanced greenhouse effect are taking place now. Hansen noted that global temperatures have been rising steadily since the late 1800s and predicts an accelerated rise over the next decade. If computer models are correct, and "the temperature trend of the last 20 years continues for another 20 years, it will be warmer than it has been in the last 100,000 years," Hansen told a *Science News* reporter.[39]

Yet Hansen as well as other atmospheric scientists have noted that there is always the possibility that natural factors could help curb the effects of carbon dioxide, CFCs, and other greenhouse gases. The oceans, for example, are a sink or "holding place" for large amounts of carbon dioxide and may be able to absorb more of that gas than scientists now predict. Increased cloudiness brought on by a warmer climate could help moderate temperatures.

In addition, there have always been warming and cooling trends and it is possible that the hot years of the 1980s could give way to a cooler cycle. Since the late 1800s, for example, there have been fluctuations in decade averages for temperature. Although temperatures rose steadily until the 1940s, they dropped slightly over the next two decades.

Still, it appears that unless changes are made to cut back the emission of greenhouse gases, they will continue to build up in the troposphere. This in turn will indirectly "affect the abundance of stratospheric ozone . . . by modifying the temperature structure of the atmosphere and hence the rates of ozone destruction," the Ozone Trends Panel reported. Warmer temperatures in the troposphere are predicted to lead to colder temperatures in the stratosphere, which would allow ice clouds to develop beyond the polar regions, providing the surfaces for additional ozone-depleting chemical reactions to occur on a global scale. Since increased ozone loss allows more UV radiation to reach the earth, not only warming trends would continue but also the effects of harmful radiation would be enhanced.

Many atmospheric scientists and meteorologists worldwide believe that changes in ozone levels and the greenhouse warming of the earth should be treated as "one combined problem."[40] In fact, a host of environmental hazards, from acid rain to nuclear fallout, can be traced to the fact that population growth and the accompanying human activities are upsetting the natural balance of life systems on the planet. As NOAA atmospheric chemist Susan Solomon put it: "We are beginning to learn that people have an astounding capacity to affect their environment." A major question is: Can people reverse or at least slow the rapid rate of environmental damage and stress placed on life support systems?

AGREEMENTS TO PROTECT THE OZONE LAYER

Debates about the adverse effects of gaseous chemicals on the atmosphere have been going on for decades in the United States and other industrialized nations. Everyone wants clean air, but how to achieve that goal has been and will be controversial for many years because of the political and economic issues involved. Another factor in finding solutions to problems of dirty air is getting public support for protective measures that may not seem reasonable if there is little understanding that chemical reactions can create atmospheric problems.

Certainly, ozone pollution—smog—is relatively easy to comprehend. People can see and smell smog and feel its effects. But the general public cannot see the effects of stratospheric pollution on the ozone layer and must trust the findings of experts studying the atmosphere. Many people outside the scientific community, including some government regulators and representatives of some industries responsible for atmospheric pollutants, want to see absolute proof of the destructive effects of gaseous chemical compounds before they take any preventive actions. For example, until the publication of the report from the Ozone Trends Panel, representatives of the Du Pont company, the world's largest manufacturer of CFCs, had long insisted that CFCs were no real danger to the ozone layer and that such assertions were based on faulty science.

Another company, Mobil Corporation, a manufacturer of plastic foam packaging as well as other petroleum products, has opposed efforts to ban foam food packages. Mobil claims that plastic foam containers do not emit harmful elements into the air when burned. "Proper incineration of foam produces virtually nothing but harmless carbon dioxide and water vapor," Mobil has insisted.[41] Yet scientific studies show that plastic foam is one of the products that releases CFCs into the atmosphere and carbon dioxide is a gas that contributes to the greenhouse effect.

What, then, has been or can be done to save the ozone layer? How has depletion of ozone, caused by human activities in nations around the globe, been addressed on a worldwide scale?

SLOW STEPS TOWARD DOMESTIC SOLUTIONS

When atmospheric researchers Rowland and Molina announced in 1974 their theory that CFCs in aerosol (spray) cans could be destroying the ozone layer, the public reacted quickly, flooding Congress with mail and telephone calls urging a ban on CFC aerosols. The federal government sponsored a study that confirmed the hazards posed by CFCs, which led to their eventual ban of aerosol spray cans. Now spray cans contain other types of propellants, and to assure consumers that a touch of the spray valve will not add to the CFC

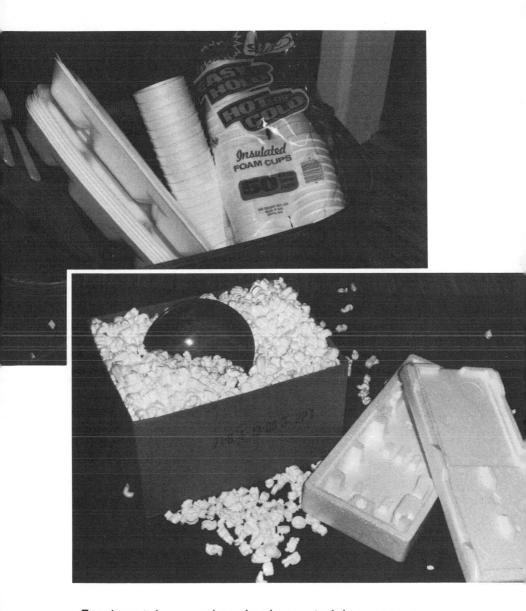

Food containers and packaging materials are some of the foam products made with chlorofluorocarbons (CFCs), gaseous chemicals that contribute to loss of ozone in the stratosphere.

burden in the stratosphere, some manufacturers have placed such labels as these on cans: "DOES NOT CONTAIN FLUOROCARBONS" or "NOT HARMFUL TO THE OZONE—NO FLUOROCARBONS."

Because of the CFC aerosol ban, Americans generally were convinced that the ozone layer had been adequately protected. The stratospheric ozone problem was "out of sight and out of mind," as far as the public consciousness was concerned. Few people

The use of CFCs in spray cans has been banned in the United States, Canada, and Scandinavian countries. U.S. manufacturers place labels on spray cans to assure consumers that propellants are not *harmful to the ozone layer.*

seemed concerned about the possibility of ozone losses.

Nevertheless, studies of stratospheric ozone loss continued, and in the late 1970s the EPA planned to ban nonaerosol use of CFCs and halons. In addition, other federal agencies were analyzing data and developing reports on the ozone-depleting effects of various halogens.

Some studies during the late 1970s and early 1980s suggested that the ozone layer might not be in as great a danger as once believed. One report, from the National Academy of Sciences, indicated that human- and naturally produced compounds, such as carbon dioxide, methane, and nitrogen oxides, in the atmosphere could help to slow down the depletion of ozone and might even raise the ozone level in the stratosphere one percent by the next century.

With all the uncertainties regarding the effects of anthropogenic chemicals in the atmosphere, there appeared to be little urgency in finding solutions to an abstract problem. Industries and government officials opposed to regulations that would require cutbacks in the use of CFCs and other ozone-depleting compounds began to call for "clear scientific evidence" that there was a serious threat to the ozone layer, and insisted that there was no justification for a CFC ban.

Federal administration views also have played a role in slowing down efforts to control CFCs and other pollutants in the atmosphere. When President Ronald Reagan took office in 1981, he and others in his administration were determined to do away with many federal government regulations of businesses and industries. Emphasis on deregulation meant that such agencies as the EPA would not actively enforce laws designed to protect the environment. In fact, Anne Gorsuch, the first EPA administrator under Reagan, belittled the ozone

depletion theory and other theories regarding air pollutants (such as acid rain and the greenhouse effect) as
scare tactics used by overly zealous environmentalists.
In addition, a worldwide economic recession at that
time lowered the demand for products containing CFCs
and also the amount of CFCs in the atmosphere. Thus
the EPA further relaxed efforts to control use of ozone-
depleting products.

By the mid-1980s, however, there was more public
pressure to protect air quality and the environment as a
whole. In the first place, scandals involving EPA officials
who protected polluters rather than the environment
had forced Gorsuch and other administrators to resign;
some EPA officials were fired. Then, in 1984, the Natural Resources Defense Council (NRDC), a private environmental group, won a lawsuit against the EPA that
required the agency to carry out provisions of the Clean
Air Act and to regulate CFCs. An economic revival had
brought an increase in the use of CFCs as well as in
emissions of carbon dioxide, methane, and nitrous oxide. Although carbon dioxide and methane tend to
buffer the effects of ozone-depleting chemicals, all of
the gases contribute to the forced greenhouse effect or
global warming. Finally, new scientific findings had
made it clear that it was no longer a matter of whether
atmospheric pollutants should be controlled but when
those controls should be put into effect.

Decisions on control regulations did not come
quickly, however, because another factor has worked
against a complete phaseout of CFCs: economics. In
1987, the director of the Alliance for Responsible Chlorofluorocarbon Policy, a group of CFC producers and
industrial users that has effectively lobbied for less restrictions on CFC use, pointed out: "We estimate the
U.S. value of goods and services relying on chlorofluorocarbons to be about $28 billion a year . . . about

715,000 jobs in the U.S. rely directly on the availability of chlorofluorocarbon compounds."[42]

CFC manufacturers have argued as well that a freeze or cutback in U.S. production of CFCs will make little difference unless there is a worldwide restriction on the chemicals. Many other nations not only make wide use of CFCs but some have increased production of these chemicals for a variety of purposes. U.S. manufacturers do not want to be singled out for cutbacks while industries in other parts of the world continue to enjoy profits from products that contain CFCs.

TOWARD INTERNATIONAL AGREEMENTS

While policies to control ozone-depleting chemicals and greenhouse gases were swinging in and out of favor in the United States, directors of the United Nations Environment Program (UNEP) called for worldwide restrictions of CFC use. Along with the United States, Japan and Western European countries, including Britain, West Germany, and France, are major producers and consumers of CFCs. In addition, developing countries and the Soviet Union have been increasing their CFC use during the latter part of the 1980s.

Over several years, the UNEP negotiated for a Convention for the Protection of the Ozone Layer. In March 1985, representatives of twenty-eight nations, including the Soviet Union, signed an agreement that essentially set up a framework for cooperative research on ozone depletion. The next step would be convincing the participating nations to sign a protocol, or a draft for a treaty, that would regulate use of CFCs and halons on a global scale.

From the time of his appointment in the mid-1980s, EPA Director Lee Thomas, in cooperation with the

UNEP, had made many efforts to bring the U.S. government and other world governments together to work out agreements on controlling global atmospheric pollutants. But conflicts erupted. The United States proposed a freeze on production of CFCs and halons with phaseouts in several stages over the next ten to fourteen years. European nations, Japan, and the Soviet Union opposed cuts in halons used for military and other purposes, and Japan did not want reductions in CFCs used in its fast-growing electronic industries.

Opposition also grew in the United States. Industry and trade specialists argued that the United States would be at a disadvantage because it had already stopped using CFC aerosols, but many other countries had not. Another major problem, opponents said, was the fact that developing effective substitutes for CFCs and halons would be costly and take time, which might allow manufacturers in other nations to gain a competitive edge, particularly if those nations were allowed longer phaseout periods than allowed for the United States.

Some federal agencies, such as the Department of Interior, were strongly against a freeze on CFCs, and some officials tried to discount the scientific evidence of ozone loss and the predicted adverse effects. In fact, U.S. Interior Secretary Donald Hodel reportedly suggested that the federal policy should be one of "personal protection"; that is, the nation could handle the effects of increased UV radiation if people would wear sunglasses and hats and stay indoors. This oversimplification of the problems presented by ozone loss brought jeers and hoots from the print and electronic media, and commentators wondered aloud whether plants and animals could be protected with sunhats and "shades."

Nevertheless, the U.S. Congress called for a reduction and eventual phaseout of CFCs and halons, and government officials in other nations also were convinced of the need for an international agreement to protect the ozone layer. On September 16, 1987, representatives from the United States, the European Community (a bloc of Western European nations that cooperate on economic matters), Japan, and other nations met in Montreal, Canada, to sign a historic United Nations treaty called the Montreal Protocol on Substances That Deplete the Ozone Layer. Two months later, the Soviet Union signed the international accord, which is designed to slow the chemical attack on stratospheric ozone.

The agreement did not become binding, however, until 1989—after ratification, or formal approval by the governing bodies of at least eleven nations that account for two-thirds of the world's use of CFCs. Mexico and the United States were the first to ratify, with the U.S. Senate voting unanimously for ratification. According to the treaty, major consumers of CFCs and halons must freeze use of these chemicals at 1986 levels of consumption. By 1999, use of CFCs must be reduced by 50 percent. The treaty also requires signatory nations to ban imports of bulk CFCs and products containing CFCs that come from nonsignatory countries.

Regulations for the use of CFCs in developing countries were less stringent since most do not have industries that manufacture CFC products. But officials of the UNEP hoped to gain cooperation from developing nations by stressing the global hazards posed by CFC compounds. If scientific reviews show that the treaty regulations do not adequately protect the global ozone layer, the Montreal agreement provides for emergency meetings of the signatory nations.

PHASING OUT CFCs AND HALONS

DU PONT TO HALT CHEMICALS THAT PERIL OZONE. The *New York Times* headlined a story that was typical of many others appearing in newspapers and national magazines during late March and early April 1988. The big news? After years of insisting that there was not strong enough scientific evidence to warrant a total ban on CFCs, E. I. du Pont de Nemours & Company (known as Du Pont) decided to phase out all production of the chemicals.

Du Pont announced it would reduce its production of CFCs at least 95 percent by the year 2000. The Wilmington, Delaware firm "said it was taking the action, which would go well beyond its previous commitment only to reduce output of the chemicals, because of new scientific evidence that the threat to the atmospheric ozone layer was worse than had been thought," the *New York Times* reported.[43]

Du Pont urged other CFC-producing companies to seriously consider the new scientific evidence presented by NASA's Ozone Trends Panel in March 1988, and to help eliminate the use of ozone-depleting chemicals. The company also called for "additional global limitations" on the production and use of CFCs and noted that substitute products were being developed.

CFC SUBSTITUTES

The Montreal agreement called for specific limits on chemical compounds found to be the most destructive of stratospheric ozone, including the CFC compounds 11, 12, 113, and the halons 1211 and 1301. The major usage of these compounds, amount of consumption in the United States and worldwide (based on the EPA's 1985 figures), and known atmospheric lifetimes are listed below.

According to a *Science News* magazine report, manufacturers of CFCs and halons are using two

Chemical	Use in millions kg U.S.	World	Lifetime in years	Primary Use
CFC 11	79.7	368.3	64	blowing bubbles into foam for furniture, refrigeration
CFC 12	136.9	455.0	108	air conditioning, refrigeration, blowing bubbles into rigid foam for food containers and insulation
CFC 113	68.5	177.0	88	cleaning solvent
Halon 1211	2.8	7.1	25	portable fire extinguishers
Halon 1301	3.5	7.0	110	total-room fire extinguishers

methods to develop substitute products that will not be a threat to the ozone layer. One method involves changing the common molecular structure of CFCs "by sticking a disruptive hydrogen atom into the stable arrangement of chlorine and fluorine. Because these new molecules are less stable, they break up in the lower atmosphere and are less liable to reach the stratosphere where they can do harm."[44]

Some CFC compounds that are less harmful to the ozone layer are already being marketed. The Du Pont company is producing HCFC 22 (or CFC 22) as a replacement for CFC 12 that has commonly been used in the manufacture of foam containers for the fast food industry and in refrigerants, particularly motor vehicle air conditioners.

However, the Motor Vehicle Manufacturers Association (MVMA) noted that in spite of the fact that CFC 22 is about 75 percent less destructive of ozone than CFC 12, motor vehicle air conditioning systems would have to be redesigned to use CFC 22 efficiently. Most of the CFC 22 compounds are used in sealed refrigerators and stationary air conditioning systems. Air conditioning systems in motor vehicles include hoses and connections that are not perfectly sealed.

The CFC 22 air conditioners operate at much higher pressure than present mobile air conditioners. Thus "carmakers would have to design and build new compressors with expensive high-strength flexible hoses. Heavy-duty batteries would be needed to supply increased power," according to a report in *Fortune*. The magazine also quoted a General Motors executive who said that retooling to use CFC 22 air conditioners would cost the company more than $600 million.[45]

Manufacturers have been reluctant to invest such large sums in research and development of mobile air conditioners that would use CFC 22 because this product, too, may be regulated or banned in the future as a hazard to the ozone layer. Motor vehicle manufacturers and other industrial users see more promise in development of alternative products that do not contain chlorine or bromine—the second method chemical companies are using to combat the CFC and halon threats.

For example, Petroferm, a chemical company with headquarters in Fernandina Beach, Florida, has produced a product called Bioact EC 7, which is made from crushed orange peels and is a terpene hydrocarbon that contains no chlorine. It will replace CFC 113 solvents, and is being used by such companies as American Telephone and Telegraph (AT&T) to clean computer circuit boards. However, the compound is similar to turpentine and presents a fire hazard not found in CFCs.

Pennwalt Corporation of Philadelphia has produced a foam-blowing agent called HCFC 141b that is also free of compounds that destroy ozone. Pennwalt, as well as other chemical companies, plans to market the compound commercially. Since HCFC 141b is a byproduct of another chemical process, production on a broad scale could take place within the decade.

Other chlorine-free hydrocarbon compounds are HCFC 123 and HFC 134a, which are currently undergoing testing. Du Pont and several other chemical companies expect to produce HCFC 123 as their foam-blowing agent, replacing CFC 11 used primarily to produce rigid foams for building and refrigerator insulation and soft foams for seat cushions. The HFC 134a compound also would be used in existing mobile air conditioning systems without major engineering changes.

In a rare form of international cooperation, fourteen chemical companies, including Du Pont and Allied-Signal in the United States, the British ICI Company,

Hoechst of West Germany, and Japan's Asahi Glass, are working together to determine the toxicity of HCFC 123 and HFC 134a. The companies are sharing the estimated $4 million costs of the tests, which may run until the mid-1990s. The importance of the toxicology tests was underscored in 1987 when Du Pont found that one substitute solvent called 132b caused sterility in male animals and thus was not considered a safe replacement for CFC solvents.

So far there are no substitutes for halons used to put out fires. The chemicals are especially valuable for extinguishing fires in such places as museums, computer installations, and rare book libraries. Halon gases when discharged create a visible fog but dissipate quickly and do not leave a residue. Such compounds not only put out the fire but protect sensitive equipment such as computers that could be "gummed up" by powdery fire extinguishing agents or damaged by moisture from liquid-type extinguishers.

Since most of the halons produced are stored in tanks waiting to be used, they are not, at that stage, a threat to the ozone layer. But large amounts of halons are released during training exercises when fire extinguishers are fully discharged. Changes in testing procedures—using other fire extinguishing agents in place of halons for training—and the development of new fire fighting equipment that does not use as much of the chemicals will help reduce halon emissions.

Cutting down on misuse or inappropriate use of portable halon fire extinguishers would help reduce emissions also. A former fire fighter and owner of a fire extinguisher business in the Midwest gave an example: "I had to refill a ten-pound halon extinguisher that was installed to protect computer-operated machinery in a manufacturing plant. Workers had used the thing to put out a grass fire. Water certainly would have been just as or more effective. In other cases, people have simply played with fire extinguishers—discharging them just to see what comes out—and never considering the consequences."

OTHER WAYS TO
REDUCE OZONE-DEPLETING
EMISSIONS

While chemical companies work on research and development of new products that will replace halons and CFCs, some industries are looking at other means for cutting back on gaseous emissions that have damaging effects on the ozone layer. One example is a new type of technology for refrigeration. According to a report in *Business Week,* research scientists in the United States and Japan "are developing devices that rely on hydrogen and nickel-alloy 'sponges.' The units work because the sponges release and reabsorb hydrogen. When hydrogen is released, the metal cools off, chilling air that flows over it."[46]

In other efforts, manufacturers are seeking ways to redesign mobile air conditioners so that there are fewer joints and tighter seals and valves, which would cut back on CFC emissions. CFCs also escape from mobile air conditioners during servicing, but if the coolant is recycled rather than allowed to evaporate, leakage of CFCs can be prevented. Removing the coolant from refrigerators and air conditioners before they are scrapped is another way to prevent the release of CFCs.

The electronics industry is also looking at methods for reducing CFC emissions. Until safe substitutes are available, a system may be designed to capture and reuse CFCs in cleaning solvents. Also, diluted CFC cleaning products could reduce the amount of ozone-depleting compounds in the atmosphere.

Some manufacturers of rigid and soft foam products are turning to pentane as a blowing agent. Because of its flammability during manufacturing, however, pentane requires added fire preventive measures. Pentane is also used in aerosol sprays. When it is mixed with a deodorant or other water-based substance, the fire hazard is eliminated.

Builders who depend on CFC-produced rigid foam insulation for new construction and remodeling projects

Foam board for home insulation is another product made with CFCs.

have found other difficulties with substitute products. For example, materials such as fiberglass and cellulose do not insulate as well as CFC foams, and various plastic materials increase fire hazards.

Still, a variety of businesses that use products manufactured with CFCs, such as foam packaging for foods, have begun to cut back on their purchases of CFC containers. One well-publicized example is McDonald's. In August 1987, the company announced that it would phase out CFC-produced styrofoam packaging and use another type of container manufactured without the use of ozone-depleting chemicals.

WHAT—IN
THE WORLD—
CAN WE DO?

McDonald's decision to discontinue use of CFC-produced foam containers is partially the result of a nationwide "McToxics Campaign" conducted by the Citizens Clearinghouse for Hazardous Wastes (CCHW), based in Arlington, Virginia. The campaign began when CCHW representatives and Senator Robert Stafford of Vermont wrote to McDonald's asking the company to stop using food containers made with CFCs. McDonald's quickly announced that it would instruct suppliers to phase out CFC-produced foam products used in the United States. A company representative told an Associated Press reporter that McDonald's made the decision even though its "packaging represents only a minute portion of total CFC usage."

CCHW and other environmental groups and federal legislators praised the company's action, but CCHW pointed out that McDonald's foam packaging causes other waste disposal problems. In a single day, throwaway foam containers from McDonald's outlets nationwide create enough waste to fill 50,000 cubic feet in landfills and when incinerated produce huge amounts of toxic gases. Thus citizens' groups in at least half the states have organized picket lines and boycotts at McDonald's restaurants to point out the environmental and health hazards posed by foam products.

Such actions can help effect changes that will reduce threats to the global environment. But what else can a group do? Is there any way that an individual working alone can make changes?

A "GLOBAL COMMONS"

Hazards to the entire planet are so complex and solutions must be based on so many diverse factors that one person can feel her or his efforts are ineffective, even a waste of time. Nevertheless, we are living in what many have called a "global village" or a "planetary spaceship," and citizens as well as policymakers in government and industry around the world need to face the challenge of how to prevent pollution on a local, regional, national, and global scale.

Individuals can begin by learning how human activities in any part of the world can have a global impact. As EPA director Lee Thomas has put it: "The depletion of stratospheric ozone and a global warming from the 'greenhouse effect' . . . are clear examples of a 'global commons' environmental problem. All nations are responsible for contributing to recent changes in our atmosphere—although the industrially developed nations must shoulder most of the responsibility. All nations will be affected by depletion of the ozone layer and by global climate changes."[47]

People in industrialized nations also are beginning to pay attention to the many scientific reports issued since the 1970s that have described the damaging effects of acid rain. Acid deposition is not yet an environmental problem with the global scale of ozone depletion and a forced greenhouse effect (although many experts argue it soon will be), but acid rain spills over state and national boundaries. In Europe, for example, many nations have realized that industrial emissions create acid rain problems far from their sources, so at least twenty countries are coordinating efforts to control acid rain precursors.

Canadians have spent years trying to convince the U.S. government that it should pass laws to curb sulfur dioxide emissions from U.S. industries. Because of wind patterns, at least half of the U.S. emissions of sulfur dioxide create acidic deposits that fall on Canada. The sulfuric acid deposits along with nitric acids produced from motor vehicles are destroying thousands of lakes in the northeastern part of the continent. Some Canadian and U.S. lakes are now so acidic that they no longer support aquatic life—plants and fish have died. Canadian industries also are heavy polluters, with an estimated 15 percent of acid fallout from Canada polluting parts of the northeastern United States. But Canada has established emission controls that will cut its 1980 levels of sulfur dioxide emissions in half by 1994.

For nearly a decade, several members of Congress have pushed for federal legislation to control U.S. industrial emissions that produce acid rain. But not until 1988 was there much widespread support in Congress for tough acid rain regulations. Lawmakers from midwestern states, where coal-burning power plants and industries are responsible for most of the sulfur dioxide emissions in the nation, have fought laws that would require expensive cleanup measures. However, the economic losses from tourism, fishing, and lumbering in Canada and the United States, plus new scientific evidence of acid rain hazards, "is making . . . congressional resistance difficult to defend." As *U.S. News and World Report* put it: "The conviction is spreading in Washington . . . that regional economics should not determine national environmental policy."[48]

GLOBAL HOUSEKEEPING

Solutions to the acid rain problem are closely related to other pollution control efforts—reducing urban smog and global warming and destruction of the ozone layer. In short, atmospheric pollutants have to be cleaned up before any of the global and regional problems they cause can be eased or eliminated.

Although the United States has not fully supported efforts to control acid rain, the nation has often led the way in scientific research on the environment and could provide leadership in policies that would guard against environmental crises. Some lawmakers consistently have called for action even before scientists have resolved the many uncertainties regarding the causes of ozone depletion and the enhanced greenhouse effect. An example is U.S. Senator John H. Chafee of Rhode Island, chair of the Senate Subcommittee on Environmental Pollution.

Chafee has made it clear that the world cannot wait for absolute proof of environmental damage from the effects of atmospheric pollutants. As he emphasized, "There is a very real possibility that society—through ignorance or indifference, or both—is irreversibly altering the ability of our atmosphere to perform basic life support functions for the planet."[49]

Such groups as the World Resources Institute, the Natural Resources Defense Council, the Environmental Defense Fund, the Sierra Club, Friends of the Earth, the Clean Air Coalition, and the National Wildlife Federation have kept up steady campaigns to alert the public about air pollution hazards and to pressure policy-makers to initiate protective measures. Individual citizens can join such action groups, or write and/or telephone legislators and other civic leaders, urging them to support domestic and international measures that will clean up the air. ³ˡ

One of the first steps would be to cut down on fossil fuels used for transportation and generating electric power. A group of atmospheric scientists summed it up during one of the international meetings held in recent years: "Reduction of coal and oil use, and energy conservation undertaken to reduce acid deposition will also reduce concentrations of greenhouse gases; reduction of emissions of CFC will protect the ozone layer and will also slow the rate of climate change."[50]

Other protective measures have been suggested in scientific reports and countless news articles published during the latter part of the 1980s. Some first steps include:

• Decreasing carbon dioxide emissions from biotic sources through an international program to stop deforestation and to replant trees on a large scale, thus holding large amounts of carbon dioxide that would otherwise be released into the atmosphere.

• Increasing energy efficiency in order to cut back on carbon dioxide emissions from fossil fuel combustion, the major contributor to the greenhouse effect. This would mean encouraging conservation by applying current technology that greatly reduces kilowatt-hours used and maintains electrical energy needed for such purposes as refrigeration, lighting, and operating appliances and machinery.

• Supporting efforts to develop renewable energy sources, such as solar energy, wind, and hydropower, which also helps to cut back on fossil fuel use. A related option may be increasing the use of nuclear power, which produces no greenhouse gases or acidic deposits. Environmentalists and others have long opposed nuclear power plants because of the dangers of nuclear fallout from meltdowns and the problem of how to dispose of hazardous nuclear wastes. But recently some critics of nuclear energy have proposed that developing better designed and smaller reactors may be one alternative to doing nothing about the buildup of greenhouse gases from fossil fuels.

Nuclear power, supplied by this plant on the shores of Lake Michigan in northern Illinois, is one controversial alternative to heavy dependence on fossil fuels for the production of energy.

• Applying new and available technology that would use natural gas to produce electricity. Although natural gas emits carbon dioxide, it produces half the amount that coal does in generating energy and does not add to the problem of acidic deposition.

• Promoting the development of energy-efficient mass transit systems around the world, and the development of alcohol and hydrogen fuels for motor vehicles to reduce carbon monoxide and ozone pollution in urban areas as well as to cut back on nitrogen oxides that contribute to smog and acid rain.

• Developing and using products that do not contain CFCs, immediately doing away with frivolous CFC applications, such as in aerosols, fast food containers, egg cartons, and other packaging materials—all of which have readily available substitutes.

• Requiring various industries to prepare environmental impact statements that show their activities do not contribute to ozone depletion and global warming.

• Regulating long-term construction projects (such as highways and development of agricultural land) so that possible climate change and sea level rise are considered in overall plans.

• Increasing scientific research on the potential hazards of atmospheric pollution.

• Bringing together coalitions of people, including scientists, lawmakers, manufacturers, environmentalists, and citizens in a variety of other occupations, to support broad international agreements for controlling precursors to acid rain, smog, greenhouse gases, and chemicals that react to destroy the ozone layer.

IN YOUR OWN BACKYARD

Supporting environmental protection policies is one form of action you can take, but like many others concerned about the fate of the planet, you may wonder about more personal, more direct approaches.

Since dry-cleaning solvents release CFCs into the atmosphere, you could buy and wear clothing that is made from washable fabrics. You can also buy furniture products (a mattress or couch, for example) and food in containers that are not made with CFC foam. A home fire extinguisher does not have to contain halon— buy the type filled with a more environmentally safe chemical.

If the air conditioner in the family car needs service, ask the mechanic to check the hoses and replace them if they leak and to drain the coolant into a container that can be sealed so CFCs are not released by evaporation. When a refrigerator or home air conditioner needs to be discarded, find out if there is a safe way to remove the coolant before the appliance is smashed in a scrap metal yard or landfill.

Energy conservation is one action that almost everyone can undertake. During times of oil shortages, people have been well aware of the need to conserve fuel, whether used to operate motor vehicles or machinery or for heating or cooling. But it is more difficult to reduce the use of an air conditioner, cut back on home heating or use of the family car if there is little understanding about the need for such measures. On the other hand, if you could join with millions of people across the nation in conservation efforts designed to protect the environment from atmospheric pollutants, fossil fuel consumption—and the release of hazardous chemical substances—would certainly decrease.

BEING A CARETAKER

Whatever each of us can do to protect our global commons, it seems crucial to begin those efforts now. Many people have scoffed at the various projections of climate change, sometimes putting those predictions in the same category as Chicken Little's warning that the sky was falling. But scientists, policymakers, citizens' and environmental groups worldwide have repeatedly emphasized that unless action is taken to curb atmospheric pollutants, the heirs of the 1980s generation will be struggling in 2020 and beyond with a vastly warmer world climate and environmental changes that have never been experienced before. Those of us living today have to ask whether we have the right to so pollute the atmosphere that people fifty to one hundred years from now will have to deal with the disastrous consequences—including increased droughts, expansion of desert areas, flooded coastal lands from rising sea levels, lower crop yields, more and more victims of cancer and other diseases, and on and on.

"Obviously, no single step is going to solve the multitude of problems associated with [atmospheric pollutants]," wrote Senator Chafee. "But we must not let the enormity of the task keep us from taking a series of small steps. . . . Tough choices need to be made and we should start what promises to be a long, sometimes frustrating process of making policy choices and regulatory decisions. . . . Present and future generations of all life-forms depend on our making the right choices."[51]

Finally, to use a much-quoted phrase: "We are all in this together." All of us need to work in our own particular ways to be caretakers of the earth.

SOURCE NOTES

CHAPTER ONE

1. W. L. Chameides et al., "The Role of Biogenic Hydrocarbons in Urban Photochemical Smog: Atlanta as a Case Study," *Science,* 16 September 1988, 1473–1475.
2. Louis Harris, *Inside America* (New York: Vintage Books, 1987), 249.

CHAPTER TWO

3. United States Environmental Protection Agency, *Ozone in the Lower Atmosphere: A Threat to Health and Welfare.* (Washington, D.C.: author, December 1986).
4. As reported in Joanne Silberner, "How a Breath of Fresh Air Can Hurt You," *U.S. News & World Report,* 29 August–5 September 1988, 100.
5. U.S. EPA, *Ozone in the Lower Atmosphere.*
6. Kathlyn Gay, *Silent Killers* (New York: Franklin Watts, 1988).
7. U.S. EPA, *Ozone in the Lower Atmosphere.*
8. "At Issue: Air Pollution and Forest Health: Three Perspectives," *American Forests* (November/December 1987): 14–15, 55.

9. Volker A. Mohnen, "The Challenge of Acid Rain," *Scientific American* 259 (August 1988): 30–38.

10. "An AFA White Paper: The Forest Effects of Air Pollution," *American Forests* (November/December 1987): 37–44.

11. Peter B. Reich and Robert G. Amundson, "Ambient Levels of Ozone Reduce Net Photosynthesis in Tree and Crop Species," *Science,* 1 November 1985, 566–570.

12. Bernhard, Prinz, "Causes of Forest Damage in Europe," *Environment* 29 (November 1987): 11–15, 32–37.

CHAPTER THREE

13. From a U.S. General Accounting Office briefing report to members of Congress on "Efforts to Control Ozone in Areas of Illinois, Indiana, and Wisconsin." January 1988, p. 13.

14. Richard Ossias, "EPA, Ozone Pollution, and the Law," *EPA Journal* (October 1987): 21.

15. Dick Russell, "L.A. Air," *The Amicus Journal* (Summer 1988): 10–20.

16. From an *Alcohol Update* interview with Gary Whitten, who recently completed a study, sponsored by the Renewable Fuels Foundation, on the impact of ethanol-blended gasoline. The interview was published in a bulletin dated May 16, 1988.

17. See a U.S. General Accounting Office briefing report to members of Congress on "Efforts to Control Ozone in Areas of Illinois, Indiana, and Wisconsin." January 1988, p. 22.

18. A published interview with J. Craig Potter, an EPA administrator who answered questions about ozone pollution. *EPA Journal* (October 1987): 8.

CHAPTER FOUR

19. Ralph J. Cicerone, "Changes in Stratospheric Ozone," *Science,* 3 July 1987, 36.

20. From a summary of these early investigations included in chapters 1 and 2 of John Gribbin, *The Hole in the Sky: Man's Threat to the Ozone Layer* (Toronto, New York, London: Bantam Books, 1988).

21. Richard A. Kerr, "Taking Shots at Ozone Hole Theories," *Science,* 14 November 1986, 817–818.

22. Richard S. Stolarski, "The Antarctic Ozone Hole," *Scientific American* 258 (January 1988): 35–36.

23. Stefi Weisburd, "The Ozone Hole, Dynamically Speaking," *Science News,* 29 November 1986, 344–346.

24. From "Statement for the Record of Dr. Daniel L. Albritton" before subcommittees of the Committee on Environment and Public Works, United States Senate, 27 October 1987.

25. From "Stratospheric Ozone: The State of the Science and NOAA's Current and Future Research." National Oceanic and Atmospheric Administration, 31 July 1987.

CHAPTER FIVE

26. From a telephone interview with Susan Solomon at NOAA's Aeronomy Laboratory in Boulder, Colorado.

27. *Executive Summary of the Ozone Trends Panel.* Washington, D.C.: 1988, p. 1.

28. Ibid., p. 13.

29. R. Monastersky, "Arctic Ozone: Signs of Chemical Destruction," *Science News,* 11 June 1988, 383. Also see Richard Kerr, "Evidence of Arctic Ozone Destruction," *Science,* 27 May 1988, 1144–45.

CHAPTER SIX

30. James G. Titus and Stephen R. Seidel, "Overview of the Effects of Changing the Atmosphere," in *Effects of Changes in Stratospheric Ozone and Global Climate,* vol. 1 (Washington, D.C.: United States Environmental Protection Agency, 1986), 18–19.

31. Edward A. Emmett, "Health Effects of Ultraviolet Radiation," in *Effects of Changes in Stratospheric Ozone and Global Climate,* vol. 1 (Washington, D.C.: United States Environmental Protection Agency, 1986), 139.

32. "SPF: The Sun-Profit Factor," *Newsweek,* 27 June 1988, 44.

33. Alun Anderson, "Antarctic Not the Place for Sun Worshipers," *Nature,* 5 November 1987, 2.

34. Alan S. Miller and Irving M. Mintzer, *The Sky Is the Limit: Strategies for Protecting the Ozone Layer,* res. rep. no. 3 (Washington, D.C.: World Resources Institute, 1986), 12.

35. Carl Sagan, "A Piece of the Sky Is Missing," *Parade* (11 September 1988): 10–15.

36. Daniel J. Dudek and Michael Oppenheimer, "The Implications of Health and Environmental Effects for Policy," in *Effects of Changes in Stratospheric Ozone and Global Climate,* vol. 1 (Washington, D.C.: United States Environmental Protection Agency, 1986), p. 371.

37. James G. Titus and Stephen R. Seidel, "Overview of the Effects of Changing the Atmosphere," in *Effects of Changes in Stratospheric Ozone and Global Climate,* vol. 1 (Washington, D.C.: United States Environmental Protection Agency, 1986), 8.

38. Jerry Bishop, "New Culprit Is Indicted in Greenhouse Effect: Rising Methane Level," *Wall Street Journal,* 24 October 1988, 1, 10.

39. Richard Monastersky, "Has the Greenhouse Taken Effect?" *Science News,* 30 April 1988, 282. See also "Scientist Says Greenhouse Warming Is Here," *Science News,* 2 July 1988, 4.

40. Ibid., 11.

CHAPTER SEVEN

41. From a display ad in *The New York Times,* 18 February 1988.

42. From a Chemical Manufacturers Association publication, *Chemecology* 16 (October 1987): 4.

CHAPTER EIGHT

43. Philip Shabecoff, "Du Pont to Halt Chemicals That Peril Ozone," *New York Times,* 25 March 1988, sec. A, A 20.

44. Richard Monastersky, "Decline of the CFC Empire," *Science News,* 9 April 1988, 234–236.

45. Stuart Gannes, "A Down-to-Earth Job: Saving the Sky," *Fortune,* 14 March 1988, 133–141.

46. "Air Conditioners That Won't Monkey with the Ozone Layer," *Business Week,* 25 April 1988, 131.

CHAPTER NINE

47. Lee Thomas, "Global Environmental Change: The EPA Perspective," in *Effects of Changes in Stratospheric Ozone*

and Global Climate, vol. 1 (Washington, D.C.: United States Environmental Protection Agency, 1987), 27–29.

48. "Yes, They Mind If We Smoke," *U.S. News & World Report,* 25 July 1988, 43–46.

49. John H. Chafee, "Our Global Environment: The Next Challenge," in *Effects of Changes in Stratospheric Ozone and Global Climate,* vol. 1 (Washington, D.C.: United States Environmental Protection Agency, 1987), 59.

50. As quoted in Gus Speth, "The Policy Context," in *Effects of Changes in Stratospheric Ozone and Global Climate,* vol. 1 (Washington, D.C.: United States Environmental Protection Agency, 1987), 335–340.

51. Chafee, "Our Global Environment, 61–62.

ORGANIZATIONS
TO CONTACT

Acid Rain Foundation
1630 Blackhawk Hills
St. Paul, MN 55122

Air Pollution Control Association
P.O. Box 2861
Pittsburgh, PA 15230

Chemical Manufacturers Association
2501 M St. N.W.
Washington, DC 20037

Environmental Action Coalition
625 Broadway
New York, NY 10012

Environmental Action Foundation
1525 New Hampshire Avenue, N.W.
Washington, DC 20036

Environmental Defense Fund
257 Park Avenue south, Suite 16
New York, New York 10016

Friends of the Earth
530 Seventh Street S.E.
Washington, DC 20003

Greenpeace, USA
1611 Connecticut Avenue, N.W.
Washington, DC 20009

National Audubon Society
950 Third Avenue
New York, New York 10022

National Clean Air Coalition
801 Pennsylvania Avenue S.E. 3rd Floor
Washington, DC 20003

National Wildlife Federation
1412 16th Street, N.W.
Washington, DC 20036

Public Citizen Health Research Group
2000 P St. N.W.
Washington, DC 20036

Sierra Club
730 Polk Street
San Francisco, CA 94109

United States Environmental Protection Agency
Public Information Center
Washington, DC 20460

World Watch Institute
1776 Massachusetts Avenue, N.W.
Washington, DC 20036

World Wildlife Fund
1255 23rd Street. N.W.
Washington, DC 20037

BIBLIOGRAPHY

BOOKS AND REPORTS

Albritton, Daniel L. *Statement for the Record Before the United States Senate* (environmental committees). Washington, D.C.: National Oceanic and Atmospheric Administration, 27 October 1987.

Albritton, Daniel L., et al. *Stratospheric Ozone: The State of the Science and NOAA's Current and Future Research.* Boulder, Colo.: NOAA, 1987.

Environmental Protection Agency. *Effects of Changes in Stratospheric Ozone and Global Climate.* Vol. 1, *Overview.* Washington, D.C.: EPA, 1986.

_____. *Ozone in the Lower Atmosphere: A Threat to Health and Welfare.* Washington, D.C.: EPA, 1986.

Gay, Kathlyn. *Acid Rain.* New York: Franklin Watts, 1983.

_____. *The Greenhouse Effect.* New York: Franklin Watts, 1986.

Global Tropospheric Chemistry Panel. *Global Tropospheric Chemistry.* Washington, D.C.: National Academy Press, 1984.

Goldsmith, Edward, and Nicholas Hildyard, eds. *The Earth Report: The Essential Guide to Global Ecological Issues.* Los Angeles: Price Stern Sloan, 1988.

General Accounting Office. *Air Pollution: Efforts to Control Ozone in Areas of Illinois, Indiana, and Wisconsin.* Washington, D.C.: GAD, 1988.

Gribbin, John. *Future Weather and the Greenhouse Effect.* New York: Delta/Eleanor Friede, 1982.

————. *Hole in the Sky: Man's Threat to the Ozone Layer.* New York: Bantam Books, 1988.

Miller, Alan S., and Irving Mintzer. *Strategies for Protecting the Ozone Layer,* Res. Rep. No. 3. Washington, D.C.: World Resources Institute, 1986.

Nierenberg, William A., et al. *Changing Climate: Report of the Carbon Dioxide Assessment Committee.* Washington, D.C.: National Academy Press, 1983.

Schneider, Stephen H., and Randi Londer. *The Coevolution of Climate and Life.* San Francisco: Sierra Club Books, 1984.

Watson, Robert T., et al. *Executive Summary of the Ozone Trends Panel.* Washington, D.C.: National Aeronautic and Space Administration, 1988.

NEWSPAPERS & PERIODICALS

Adler, Jerry, with Mariana Gosnell, Karen Springen, and Nikki Finke Greenberg. "The Dark Side of the Sun." *Newsweek,* 9 June 1986, 60–64.

"An AFA White Paper: The Forest Effects of Air Pollution." *American Forests,* November/December 1987, 37–44.

"Air Conditioners That Won't Monkey with the Ozone Layer." *Business Week,* 25 April 1988, 131.

Anderson, Alun. "Antarctic Not the Place for Sun Worshippers." *Nature,* 5 November 1987, 2.

Anderson, Earl V. "EPA Is Set to Propose Tough Fuel Volatility Regulations." *Chemical & Engineering News,* 6 July 1987, 7–13.

Beck, Melinda, with Mary Hager. "More Bad News for the Planet." *Newsweek,* 28 March 1988, 63.

Begley, Sharon, with Bob Cohn. "The Silent Summer: Ozone Loss and Global Warming: A Looming Crisis." *Newsweek,* 23 June 1986, 64–66.

Begley, Sharon, with Mary Hager and Dorothy Wang. "A Gaping Hole in the Sky." *Newsweek,* 11 July 1988, 21–23.

Begley, Sharon, with Mark Miller and Mary Hager. "Inside the Greenhouse: Heat Waves." *Newsweek,* 11 July 1988, 16–20.

Bishop, Jerry E. "New Culprit Is Indicted in Greenhouse Effect: Rising Methane Level." *Wall Street Journal,* 24 October 1988, A1, A10.

Bowman, Kenneth P. "Global Trends in Total Ozone." *Science,* 1 January 1988, 48–50.

Boyle, Robert H. "Forecast for Disaster." *Sports Illustrated,* 16 November 1987, 80–92.

Brasseur, Guy. "The Endangered Ozone Layer." *Environment,* January/February 1987, 6–11, 39–45.

Brodeur, Paul. "Annals of Chemistry: In the Face of Doubt." *The New Yorker,* 9 June 1986, 70–87.

Browne, Malcolm W. "New Ozone Threat: Scientists Fear Layer Is Eroding at North Pole." *The New York Times,* 11 October 1988, C1, C11.

Cicerone, Ralph J. "Changes in Stratospheric Ozone." *Science,* 3 July 1987, 35–42.

Citron, Michelle. "The Hole Truth." *Discover,* January 1988, 72–73.

Crawford, Mark. "Landmark Ozone Treaty Negotiated." *Science,* 25 September 1987, 1557.

————. "Ozone Plan Splits Administration." *Science,* 29 May 1987, 1052–1053.

————. "United States Floats Proposal to Help Prevent Ozone Depletion." *Science,* 21 November 1986, 927–929.

"Death of Plankton Could Signal Ozone Loss." *Environment,* September 1986, 23.

Doniger, David D. "Politics of the Ozone Layer." *Issues in Science and Technology,* Spring 1988, 86–92.

"EPA Attacks Vapor Villain." *Motor Trend,* November 1987, 44.

"Environment and the Public's Purses." *Nature,* 2 June 1988, 381.

Evans, Harold. "The Great Procrastinators." *U.S. News & World Report,* 11 July 1988, 67.

Gannes, Stuart. "A Down-to-Earth Job: Saving the Sky." *Fortune,* 14 March 1988, 133–141.

"Global Ozone Trends Reassessed." *Nature,* 17 March 1988, 201.

Graf, Tom. "Front Rangers Breathe Easier." *Sierra,* March/ April 1988, 27–28.

Green, Bill. "Policies on Global Warming and Ozone Depletion." *Environment,* April 1987, 5, 45.

Gribbin, John. "The Ozone Layer." *New Scientist,* 5 May 1988, 1–4.

Hanson, David J. "Clean Air Goals Raising Concerns About Pollution Control." *Chemical & Engineering News,* 28 March 1988, 24–26.

"The Heat Is On: Chemical Wastes Spewed into the Air Threaten the Earth's Climate." *Time,* 19 October 1987, 58–63.

Hileman, Bette, and Wil Lepkowski. "Ohio, New York Agree On Acid Rain Proposal." *Chemical & Engineering News,* 13 June 1988, 9–10.

Hoppe, Richard. "Ozone: Industry Is Getting Its Head Out of the Clouds." *Business Week,* 13 October 1986, 110.

Ivey, Mark, with Ronald Grover. "Alcohol Fuels Move Off the Back Burner." *Business Week,* 29 June 1987, 100–101.

Johnston, Kathy. "First Steps in Ozone Protection Agreed." *Nature,* 17 September 1987, 189.

Kerr, Richard. "Stratospheric Ozone Is Decreasing." *Science,* 25 March 1988, 1489–1491.

————. "Evidence of Arctic Ozone Destruction." *Science,* 27 May 1988, 1144–1145.

————. "Halocarbons Linked to Ozone Hole." *Science,* 5 June 1987, 1182–1183.

————. "Has Stratospheric Ozone Started to Disappear?" *Science,* 10 July 1987, 131–132.

————. "Is the Greenhouse Here?" *Science,* 5 February 1988, 559–561.

————. "The Deepest Antarctic Ozone Hole Ever Seen." *Science,* 8 January 1988, 146.

————. "Winds, Pollutants Drive Ozone Hole." *Science,* 9 October 1987, 156–158.

Lemonick, Michael D., and Edwin M. Reingold. "Culprits of the Stratosphere." *Time,* 21 September 1987, 57.

Lewis, Jack. "Finding Technologies to Control Ozone Pollution." *EPA Journal,* October 1987, 15–17.

Lindley, David. "Ozone Hole Deeper Than Ever." *Nature,* 8 October 1987, 473.

Luoma, Jon R. "The Human Cost of Acid Rain." *Audubon,* July 1988, 16–29.

Maddox, John. "The Great Ozone Controversy." *Nature,* 10 September 1987, 101.

————. "Jumping the Greenhouse Gun." *Nature,* 7 July 1988, 9.

Miller, Mark. "Not So Bad After All? Nuclear Power Revisited." *Newsweek,* 25 July 1988, 65.

Mohnen, Volker A. "The Challenge of Acid Rain." *Scientific American,* August 1988, 30–38.

Monastersky, Richard. "Decline of the CFC Empire." *Science News,* 9 April 1988, 234–236.

————. "Has the Greenhouse Taken Effect?" *Science News,* 30 April 1988, 282.

————. "Ozone Accord Draws Praise and Concern." *Science News,* 26 September 1987, 196–197.

————. "Scientist Says Greenhouse Warming Is Here." *Science News,* 2 July 1988, 4.

————. "Arctic Ozone: Signs of Chemical Destruction." *Science News,* 11 June 1988, 383.

Nilsson, Sten, and Peter Duinker. "The Extent of Forest Decline in Europe." *Environment,* November 1987, 4–9, 30–31.

Norton, Robert. "Yes, They Mind If We Smoke." *U.S. News & World Report,* 25 July 1988, 43–45.

"The Ozone Layer." *Chemecology,* October 1987, 2–4.

Peterson, Cass. "High Anxiety." *Sierra,* January/February 1988, 34–39.

Pope, Carl. "Once More, with Compliance." *Sierra,* September/October 1987, 34–38.

Postel, Sandra. "Life, the Great Chemistry Experiment." *Natural History,* April 1987, 42–48.

Prinz, Bernhard. "Causes of Forest Damage in Europe." *Environment,* November 1987, 11–15, 32–37.

Raloff, Janet. "Deforestation: Major Threat to Ozone?" *Science News,* 23 August 1986, 119.

Reich, Peter B., and Robert G. Amundson. "Ambient Levels of Ozone Reduce Net Photosynthesis in Tree and Crop Species." *Science,* 1 November 1985, 566–570.

Reisch, Marc, and Pamela Zurer. "CFC Production: Du Pont Seeks Total Phaseout." *Chemical & Engineering News,* 4 April 1988, 4–5.

Russel, Milton. "Environmental Protection for the 1990s and Beyond." *Environment,* September 1987, 12–15, 34–38.

Russell, Dick. "L.A. Air." *The Amicus Journal,* Summer 1988, 10–20.

Sagan, Carl. "A Piece of the Sky is Missing." *Parade,* 11 September 1988, 10–15.

Savage, Harlin. "Hill Moves to Break Clean Air Stalemate." *The National Voter,* June 1988, 2.

"Scientists Probe Thinning of Ozone." *Chemecology,* December 1986/January 1987, 5–6.

Shaw, Robert W. "Air Pollution by Particles." *Scientific American,* August 1987, 96–103.

Shell, Ellen Ruppel. "Solo Flights into the Ozone Hole Reveal Its Causes." *Smithsonian Magazine,* 142–156.

_____. "Watch This Space." *Omni,* 36–42, 80–81.

_____. "Weather Versus Chemicals." *The Atlantic,* May 1987, 27–31.

Silberner, Joanne. "Layers of Complexity in Ozone Hole." *Science News,* 14 March 1987, 164.

Singer, S. Fred, and Candace Crandall. "Assessing the Threat to the Ozone." *Consumers' Research Magazine,* July 1987, 11–14.

"SPF: The Sun-Profit Factor." *Newsweek,* 27 June 1988, 44.

Starr, Douglas. "How to Protect the Ozone Layer." *National Wildlife,* December/January 1988, 26–28.

"Staving Off Dirty Air." *U.S. News & World Report,* 28 September 1987, 107.

Stolarski, Richard S. "The Antarctic Ozone Hole." *Scientific American,* January 1988, 30–36.

Strait, Donald S., and Richard E. Ayres. "High Noon for Smog Control." *Environment,* September 1987, 43–45.

Sun, Marjorie. "Tighter Ozone Standard Urged by Scientists." *Science,* 24 June 1988, 1724–1725.

Swinbanks, David. "Counting the Environmental Cost of Japan's Progress." *Nature,* 2 June 1988, 385.

Uehling, Mark D. "Missing the Deadline on Ozone." *National Wildlife,* October/November 1987, 34–37.

"We Need the Ozone Layer More Than Styrofoam." *Business Week,* 4 April 1988, 128.

Weisburd, Stefi. "Ozone Reports Stir Debate." *Science News,* 9 January 1988, 20.

_____. "The Ozone Hole, Dynamically Speaking." *Science News,* 29 November 1986, 344–346.

Wellborn, Stanley N. "Facing Life in a Greenhouse." *U.S. News & World Report,* 29 September 1986, 73–74.

"Where the World Stands on Ozone." *Nature,* 24 March 1988, 291.

Wilson, Richard D. "Alternative Fuels: Their Prospects for Fighting Smog." *EPA Journal,* October 1987, 18–19.

Woodwell, William, Jr. "The Defiled Blue Yonder." *The National Voter,* August/September 1987, 8–14.

Zurer, Pamela S. "Antarctic Ozone Hole: Complex Picture Emerges." *Chemical & Engineering News,* 2 November 1987, 22–26.

_____. "Search Intensifies for Alternatives to Ozone-Depleting Halocarbons." *Chemical & Engineering News,* 8 February 1988, 17–20.

_____. "Ozone Layer: Study Finds Alarming Global Loss." *Chemical & Engineering News,* 21 March 1988, 6–7.

_____. "Studies on Ozone Destruction Expand Beyond Antarctic." *Chemical & Engineering News,* 30 May 1988, 16–25.

INDEX

EDUCATION